Specialty Food Store Design

Specialty Food Store Design

Martin M. Pegler

VISUAL REFERENCE PUBLICATIONS, INC.

NEW YORK

Visual Reference Publications, Inc.
302 Fifth Avenue
New York, NY 10001

Distributors to the trade in the United States and Canada
Watson-Guptill Publishers
1515 Broadway
New York, NY 10036

Distributors outside the United Sates and Canada
Hearst Books International
1350 Avenue of the Americas
New York, NY 10019

Library of Congress Cataloging in Publication Data:
Specialty Food Store Design

Printed in Hong Kong
ISBN 0-934590-77-X

Designed by Dutton & Sherman

Contents

Shoppers today are smarter than ever before: they are more demanding but they are willing to spend their money to get "value". In this ever upscaling society, the shopper is seeking the unique, the different, and the "designer name" or brand name that reflects the shopper's good taste.

To accommodate the discriminating shopper, successful retailers are specializing: finding niches where they can provide the products and services for a particular shopper. This nichemanship of specializing has also flourished in the food area. Supermarkets are getting better looking but have gone beyond the conventional food emporium to become hypermarkets or mini-malls that also stock clothing, home accessories and/or appliances, video exchanges, drugs and toiletries, flowers and party supplies. As the supermarkets get bigger and bigger, the more affluent and the more educated seek out the smaller and more specialized markets and stores. It is almost the return to the comfort, the convenience and the security of a bygone era when people shopped in the corner grocery store—and each customer was called by name. There is also an awareness and an awakening: a return to the natural, the wholesome and the healthy.

Farmer's markets, organic produce shops and natural and health food stores are joined by up scaled, elegant imported specialty and gourmet take-out food stores. They are appearing in local neighborhoods, in strip centers, in malls and on Main Streets across the country. Some stores emphasize the "quality" of the product with handsome fixture and fittings, with rich materials and handsome displays and under flattering light. Others take their visual cues from the old world open markets and the small neighborhood food shops where fruits and vegetables were lovingly picked and arranged in baskets and bushels and presented as works of art. These shops do not stress volume: they present quality. Wine and liquor stores are now often combined with wine tasting rooms and candy stores continue the entertainment theme that seems to be the mantra of today's retailers.

In this volume of *Specialty Food Store Design* we have included bakeries, candy stores, wine and liquor establishments, some convenience stores and gourmet markets where the emphasis is on gourmet and wholesome foods. We have also included some "boutiques" that are appearing in supermarkets that are so well done that they could be free standing stores. Some restaurants, especially those specializing in ethnic or provincial foods, have established marketplaces or take-out food shops where the diner can shop for prepared foods, baked goods, condiments—anything that will prolong the dining experience.

Though supermarkets continue to thrive, it is the specialty and gourmet food outlets that make up the rapidly growing segment of the food industry. They provide the shopper with something extra: the feeling of making a special purchase in a unique setting that has been designed for the discerning consumer.

Martin M. Pegler

Retailers are challenged like never before to obtain a share of the consumer's dollars. To rise above the countless choices that face a prospective customer, store owners and designers increasingly are weaving an element of theater into the shopping experience. They have come to understand that each retailer is a single component in an ever-changing backdrop. Consumers want and expect not only to find the products that brought them to a store but also to be entertained.

This dynamic of the business has prompted many proprietors to embark on retail pilgrimages, traveling across town and to far away cities to see what the other guys are up to. What they are discovering is that, just as the medium of the stage is composed of a number of contrasting styles, from sparsely adorned sets to elaborate multi-scene constructions, so too do retail stores vary in the way they reach out to the shopper.

Take, for example, the display of products. A stark layout consisting of baskets of produce with a finite number of places for the eye to wander will impress an entirely different feeling on a patron than an intentionally cluttered array where one could stare at a single shelf for three minutes and still not "see" everything. Graphics, signage, color, and store layout are just a few of the other variables with which retailers are experimenting—and from a look at the beautiful photos on these pages, they are having a lot of fun.

So join us on a magic carpet ride to 75 retailers located throughout the world. As in any other pursuit, retailing is a never-ending educational process. As you travel through this book, pay attention to the ideas that might work in your own store. Here's your chance to see how your peers create truly unique environments that, sometimes more subtly than others, shape the consumer's overall experience.

Happy trails!

Edward R. Loeb

Edward Loeb

Publisher of *The Gourmet Retailer Magazine*

Hors d'Oeuvres · Appetizers · Entrees & Side Dishes

Sutton Place Gourmet

McLean, VA

DESIGN *Mark Ksiazewski, Director of Design, Sutton Pl. Gourmet*

ARCHITECTS *Anderson, Cooper, Georgelas*

PHOTOGRAPHER *Prakash Patel*

SUTTON PLACE GOURMET
McLean, Virginia

According to the designer, Mark Ksiazewski, Director of Design for the Sutton Place Gourmet Company, "Capturing the customer with color, aroma and action: that's the Sutton Place Gourmet approach to fine food retailing." Nowhere is this trinity more evident than in this new store in McLean, VA.

The space is open and airy with soaring ceilings, open sight lines, and "aisle-free" merchandising. The heart of the store is the tent covered "Hay Day Produce Market." The tent top serves as a screen for seasonally changing, mood-setting projected images. A 1950-ish tractor restates the country fair theme as it "pulls" a set of refrigerated produce bins.

The color palette for the floor, walls and ceiling ranges from copper to burgundy to sage green "creating a glowing environment accentuated by the use of halogen spotlights for crisp brightness." A supergraphic of color defines the store with lighting and color matched to the food categories: ie; the meat department is orange, burgundy, rust and purple. Jewel tones provide visual interest as well as break up the space above the departments. The departments are located under the warm cherry stained maple signs lettered with custom type. "The overall effect on the customer is to create a casual sense of warmth and well being."

Sutton Place Gourmet shoppers have access to food professionals and the open kitchen, and the wood burning ovens are emblematic of that service. Merchandise is displayed in casual groupings that invite the shopper to wander, explore, and try the products in this customer friendly arrangement. Throughout the space, it is the food that stars in the presentation.

Bluebird

Kings Road, London, England

DESIGN *CD Partnership, London, England*

Bluebird is the realization of Terence Conran's dream. Conran's own store design group, the CD Partnership, turned a much-beloved London landmark, The Bluebird Garage which was once listed as Europe's largest motor garage into an "epicurean experience" for lovers of fine foods and drink. This relic of the early 20th century has been reborn and now houses a large food market, a wine merchant, flower market, kitchen shop, traiteur, bakery and patisserie as well as an outdoor fruit and vegetable market along with a restaurant, cafe, bar and private dining club.

The tiled and rendered facade with its columned art-deco look has been restored as have the copper-lite windows that run from floor to ceiling along the front of the structure. The courtyard has been repaved in salvaged Scottish granite sets and York stone. A steel and glass canopy extends over most of the outdoor market area.

The interior is simple and functional with steel trusses supporting the roof and the first floor slab which makes this an entirely column-free ground floor. This clear, open ground floor was perfect when the space was used as a garage and

now provides a spectacular food market hall. Produce is presented in a straight-forward manner on customized display counters and shelves. Each of the five tall windows represents another department and a staff of specialists is available to assist shoppers in each area.

There are oils and spices, specially-blended teas and coffees, pastas and rice, chocolates and confectionery, as well as specialty counters for meat, poultry and game, fish and shellfish, charcuterie, dairy products and cheese. The traiteur provides restaurant quality food for dining at home. The take-out foods range from stews and casseroles to pasta and gnocchi. There are also prepackaged, ready-to-go, fish, meat and poultry dinners all set up to satisfy two.

"The Bluebird is everyone's neighborhood store but with a fundamental difference. A busy, bustling place, customers can see, smell, touch the food offering and be served from counters by staffers who really know what they are selling. A world away from the sterile environment of today's supermarkets, Bluebird is generous and friendly."

Straub's Market

Clayton, MO

DESIGN *Kiku Obata & Co., St. Louis, MO*

DESIGN TEAM *Kiku Obata, Pam Bliss, Kevin Flynn, AIA, Theresa Henrekin, Lisa Bollmann, Alissa Andres*

PHOTOGRAPHER *Cheryl Unger, Denver, CO*

"Straub's Market is a place reminiscent of an elegant yet simple past. It reminds us of our familiar roots, a time when life was less harried and people were friendlier. It's a place where the owner and butcher know your name." Since 1901, Straub Markets have served communities in Missouri and recently Kiku Obata & Co. was commissioned to update and remodel the produce area of the Clayton location—"creating a fresh, contemporary look while maintaining that sentimental charm and casual elegance that makes Straub's Market a St. Louis icon."

The materials, colors and finishes used by the designers in the 1350 sq. ft. produce area are "reminiscent of a timeless, elegant age." The classic style is "exaggerated" and elements of sentiment and surprise were added. At the entrance to this department, special finishes were applied to found furniture (reclaimed and recycled) to create flexible merchandising. "These cross-selling fixtures add

additional appeal to items normally stocked in the aisles." Custom designed, curved fixtures fit around the circular staircase. Piled high fresh fruits and vegetables sit atop the dark, distressed table tops and contrast with the gift wicker baskets on the soft pink nesting tables.

Accentuating the line of the curving stairway is a soffit on whose outer edge is "a delightful verse comparing arrangements of fruit to artistic moments" while inside is a potpourri of produce images.

Throughout, the designers have taken full advantage of display opportunities; lemons and limes piled up in concrete urns, oranges in wire bushel baskets, red apples in white glazed pottery and melons and squashes in pale, pink wood crates. "All of these images, colors and textures appeal to the senses to convey Straub's casual atmosphere."

Grassroots

Soho, New York, NY

DESIGN   *Bogdanow Partners, Architects P.C., New York, NY*

DESIGN TEAM   *Larry Bogdanow, Tom Schweitzer, Florianne Grembine, Eizo Atarashi*

CLIENT   *Larry & Michael Fox*

GRAPHICS   *Louise Fili, New York, NY*

PHOTOGRAPHER   *Paul Warchol*

The 7200 sq. ft. store, on lower Broadway in New York City, is in one of the many historic cast iron front buildings. Grassroots is a natural foods market offering organically grown produce, natural food groceries, gourmet prepared foods, vitamins and personal care accessories. The successful design of Grassroots is based on the balance of old and new: Bogdanow left many of the building's architectural interior and exterior elements intact while adding everything necessary to make the space a state-of-the-art food store.

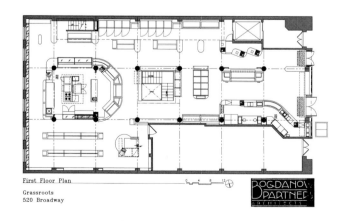

First Floor Plan
Grassroots
520 Broadway

The 16 ft. ceilings over the 4500 sq. ft. ground floor add to the impression of an open marketplace. The front end of the store is filled with the enticing color of citrus, tropical and seasonal fruits in baskets and in the open refrigerated cases. On the right wall more baskets contain a variety of fresh vegetables and there is a special case for herbs and greens. A juice/coffee bar, visible from the street—fills the left side of the store along with etageres displaying muffins and other baked goods.

The store features maple plank floors, Corinthian columns and a skylight along the rear wall. Shelves were installed from 9-13 ft. from the floor to allow for the generous levels of visible inventory. Also fitted into the space are a free-standing central salad bar, additional refrigerator cases on either side of the store and the vitamins and health preparations stocked in the left back alcove.

The visual point of the rear of the store is the prepared foods area with round cases filled with cheeses, casseroles, fish, olives, salads, entrees and fresh baked breads. A copper fascia, suspended from the ceiling, repeats the curve of the counter and halogen spots sparkle along the length of the copper band.

Kafer

Munich, Germany

When one speaks of great food shops—of gourmet food emporiums—around the world, certain names are sure to appear. One must list Fauchon in Paris, Harrod's Food Hall in London, Peck's in Milan, Ka De We in Berlin—and Kafer in Munich.

Located in a historic building on Prinzregentstrasse, Kafer has five floors devoted to the presentation of gourmet prepared foods and packaged delicacies from around the world. The catering service can "whip up" a sensational dinner for up to 2000 people anywhere in the world and several of Munich's opera houses and theaters serve Kafer prepared foods.

Everywhere there is wood, tile, marble, mirror, glints of brass and crystal—and rich and antique furniture. Whether it is in the produce area where Bavarian grown produce appears on display alongside exotic fruits and vegetables flown in daily or in the Delicatssen shop where the shopper can select from hundreds of meats, fish, condiments, jams, jellies and confectionery—the presentation is always flawless. There are specialty areas within this food emporium like a butcher shop, a fish/shellfish area with fresh displays of catches, and even a wine cellar with a gigantic selection. Like the other shops within the shop, the Wine Cellar is staffed by knowledgeable specialists ready to suggest, advise or even select for the overwhelmed customer. The bakery offers over 130 different baked items daily and will even custom bake from the patron's own recipe.

The motto at Kafer is "alles is moglich"—anything is possible! No matter what the shopper may desire, his or her wish can be satisfied in this unique establishment which combines the comfort and convenience of the corner grocery store with the most exotic of gourmet palaces. One has only to ask!

Gourmet Satisfaction

Iwataya Z-Side Dept. Store,
Fukuoka, Japan

DESIGN   *Walker Group/CNI, New York, NY*

Located on the lower level of the new, multi-level department store, Iwataya Z-Side in Fukuoka is Gourmet Satisfaction, a gourmet market, bakery and wine shop.

To identify this floor, the key is "freshness": freshness and assortment. To bring the message across to the shoppers, the architects/designers used photographic compositions of products "at different sizes and positions on a background of color that communicates a rich, healthy product offering." Similar images are re-interpreted in different ways in key locations throughout the floor.

The circulation plan is simple and clear and it organizes the various product offerings in an easy-to-comprehend manner. The use of assorted tile patterns as well as specialized accent tiles on the floor "provide color and focus within a more neutral framework." To further assist the shopper moving through the floor, the ceiling structures, custom lighting fixtures, environmental graphics and the signage further animate the space and provide clear orientation and identification of products. The designers also introduced special fixtures with sculptures to add a feeling of fun and whimsy to the selling floor.

Ka De We

Berlin, Germany

DESIGN *Norbert Konnecke*

The famous food floor opened in 1956 and has become a legend. This "rendezvous for Gourmets" is on the sixth floor and can be reached by a non-stop express elevator. It is the largest food department in Europe (5,100 sq. meters) and the second largest in the world. The shopper can find 25,000 edible items here including 400 kinds of bread and 1,800 types of cheese. Each week 20,000 tons of fruit, vegetable, meat, fish and cheese are purchased and three times each week fresh fish is flown in refrigerated containers from France, Israel, Turkey and German seaports. Fruits and vegetables also come from all over the world. The most renowned French gourmet houses and master chefs have branches in the sixth floor of Ka De We. "The choice ranges from Lenotre to Fauchon and Bocuse, but also extends as far as stalls of beer and boilettes."

A newly redesigned Fresh Fish area has taken its place on Six and it sparkles with glass, gray marbled walls, and slick black cases—all highlighted and accented with gleaming brass tubing. The area is brilliant with light from rows of incandescents lined up on the ceiling. The snack area and bar are extensions of this newly renovated area with the light gray marble floor inset with black diamond designs.

Pano's Food Shop

Atlanta Fish Market,
Atlanta, GA

DESIGN   *Zakaspace, Ft. Lauderdale, FL, and*
Atlanta, GA

PRINCIPALS   *Spiros Zakas & Peter Zakas*

PROJECT DESIGNER   *Karen Hanlon*

PROJECT COORDINATOR   *Marc Geftman*

PHOTOGRAPHY   *Mark Ballogg,*
Steinkamp/Ballog Photography

Part of and yet apart from the popular seafood restaurant, Atlanta Fish Market in Atlanta, is Pano's Food Shop. Both projects were designed by Zakaspace of Ft. Lauderdale & Atlanta.

Following a trend that is becoming as popular as tee-shirt and coffee mug souvenir shops in theme restaurants are the take-out shops and mini-retail food stores evolving in some restaurant designs. Like the Atlanta Fish Market that was designed to look as though it had always been there, there is an old fashioned/old time look to this market that is housed in a large clapboard addition to the restaurant. Not only are fresh vegetable and fruits for sale as well as assorted take-out salads and prepared meals, there is a large area devoted to freshly caught, cut and prepared fish.

The floors are laid with a giant checkerboard of black and white vinyl tiles, set on a diagonal, and natural wood faced counters that complement the wood paneling.

Cracker Barrel Corner Market

Nashville, TN

DESIGN *Design Forum, Dayton, OH*

PHOTOGRAPHY *Jamie Padgett, Karant Assoc. Chicago, IL*

This unique market is a one-stop deli/grocery and restaurant where diners can either eat in or take out. The goal set for Design Form of Dayton, OH was to create a marketplace setting where customers had a choice of dining and shopping options. Mimicking an 1850s old country general store, the space is filled with nostalgic elements that provide the down country, homey look.

Bleached woods line the perimeter fascias where the food categories are indicated in graphics that appear to have been washed out by overexposure to the sun—or just faded by time. The clay tile floor, in variations of terra cotta red and brown, is not only practical but adds to the warm and friendly feeling the designers were trying to capture. Mahogany colored wall cabinets and counters contrast with the distressed wood finishes and also suggest a time that is long past.

The packaged merchandise is set out on the floor atop artfully stacked crates, barrels, and open food carts. The open plan allows shoppers to make their own traffic patterns guided by the signage and the displays of gift baskets and dry goods. The ceiling is painted a deep, dark color and seems to vanish but it also adds a sense of intimacy and provides a comfortable scale for the shoppers. Light tracks fill the dark void and spots highlight the product display and the wall signage.

Emily's Market

Phoenix, AZ

DESIGN *Design Forum, Dayton, OH*

PHOTOGRAPHY *Jamie Padgett, Karant Assoc. Chicago, IL*

Emily's Market, a new shopping concept for Circle K, hones in on today's busy American lifestyle and allows shoppers to take home "a slice of the past" with pre-prepared food—"like Mom made them."

In a space of 3000 sq. ft., Design Forum brought into reality this mixture of convenience/grocery store and gourmet deli: "the ultimate category killer in home meal replacement—Emily's Kitchen." The store's design celebrates the architecture and ambiance of a Midwestern American town of the previous century and takes color and style cues from a Mary Engelbreit-style garden. At the hub of the store is the "Market Sampler"—a central focal area stocked with fresh entrees and a menu planner to help customers with catering and meal selections.

In all, there are six departments in this red tile, white wood and black ceilinged space including take-out meals, a bakery, produce, ready-to-eat entrees, sides and vegetables, hot sandwiches and gourmet pizzas. Between the grocery items, the take-away entrees and the a la carte selections, the shopper can build and then leave with a complete custom dinner.

Old wooden barrels and warm wooden fixtures "clutter" the floor—overflowing with "take-me-home" products. On the fascia over the perimeter shelving is a series of shuttered windows of 19th century white clapboard houses that creates the illusion that the sales floor is an outdoor market square. The foliage that drips down from the black ceiling further extends the out of doors feeling. The lighting combines focusable spots with old fashioned, milk glass drop lights over the counters. Who says "cooking" can't be fun—especially when Emily does it all?

Dino's Pasta Market

Los Angeles, CA

DESIGN *Hatch Design Group, Costa Mesa, CA*

DESIGN: *Jeff Hatch*

GRAPHICS *Lisa King*

CREATIVE CONCEPT CONSULTANT
Linda Bermnan

GIFT & DISPLAY DESIGNER *Edith DeCristo*

PHOTOGRAPHER *Douglas Hill Photography,
Los Angeles, CA*

Richard Hayman and Dean Saduto have combined time honored traditions of the local neighborhood Italian market and trattoria with the American demand for a convenient "one stop" shop in their new Italian retail concept—Dino's Pasta Market. A dream team of culinary and retail professionals were brought together to make this concept work.

Jeff Hatch and his design team created the setting and the ambiance in the 2500 sq. ft. store that suggests the warmth and friendliness of the old Italian corner grocery store or maybe even a market shop in a village in Tuscany with its shelves and counters laden with local cheeses, cured hams, salamis, fresh breads and barrels of cured olives.

The design team married the vibrant colors, textures and rusticity of that traditional market store with the more abundant, cosmopolitan feeling of a Milanese gourmet food emporium. The store is designed to showcase the full line of fresh and dried pastas, antipasto, salads, cured meats, cheeses, desserts and wines. The shopper can move from one course to the next course—shopping for the meal

the way she might ordinarily shop for the basics for her pantry or refrigerator. In addition, there are fully prepared, restaurant quality meals packaged in reheatable containers, ready-to-go salads and even the cut flowers to add a festive touch to the dinner table.

Heyman and Saduto hope to establish Dino's Pasta Market as the "ultimate neighborhood Italian market" specializing in quality pasta and complementary items for home meal preparation. "We will maintain Italian culinary tradition, offer value and provide a convenient, charming and service-driven environment."

Food & Co.

Pesaro, Italy

DESIGN   *Design Studio Auguzzi, Ancona, Italy*

ART DIRECTION   *Acanto, Pesaro*

FIXTURES   *Sifa/Sinthesi, Hollywood, FL*

PHOTOGRAPHER   *Studio 33, Pesaro*

Though this shop is modern and contemporary in styling as are the fixtures designed and manufactured by Sifa, there is still a feeling of tradition and warmth inherent in the design of this charcutterie/bakery in Pesaro in Italy.

The wall system combines vertical panels of wood or accent colors with a slotted system that makes shelf placement simple and convenient. A valance extends forward on top and hides the fixture that illuminates the products displayed on the shelves. The fronts of the counters and cases can be finished in matching woods or with colored laminates and accented with borders of ceramic tiles.

The bakery area is finished with floor tiles of biscuit beige; a checkerboard of matte and shiny tiles alternating. The warm wood facing the angled counter is accented with copper tiles and a corrugated copper cornice extends out from the rear wall. An angled mirrored panel puts the breads and prepackaged materials on the uppermost shelf into view for the shopper. Natural wicker baskets and lamp shades add a "traditional" touch to the modern design.

Promoter 2

Pesaro, Italy

DESIGNER *Design Studio Auguzzi, Ancona, Italy*

ART DIRECTION *Acanto, Pesaro*

FIXTURES *Sifa/Sinthesi, Hollywood, FL*

PHOTOGRAPHER *Studio 33, Pesaro*

In contrast to the "old Italian grocery" look at Genuardi's, we complement that with this smart, modern new Italian look. This is one of three prototype stores created by and for the designers/manufacturers of Sifa refrigeration cases and Sinthesi wall and floor fixturing systems.

This store was designed to showcase the refrigerator cases in a small charcutteri/deli store in Pesaro on the eastern coast of Italy. The shop's rear wall is lined with wood panels and an adjustable shelving system. Small, low voltage lamps, lined up under the cornice, provide light for the products shown on the shelves.

The L-shaped arrangement of white molded and sculpted refrigerator cases, accented with wood veneer, serves to gracefully lead the shopper into the narrow but long shop. Biscuit colored Italian tiles are used on the floor to complement the warm and pleasant neutral look of the shop that is illuminated by incandescents.

The Genuardi Family Markets reflect a rich heritage and family tradition since the Genuardis are "passionate about food." The market environments are designed to reflect that feeling as well as showcase the food offerings for upscale customers with busy lifestyles.

The shopping experience begins with the specially-designed and merchandised Italian Market that sets the tone for the balance of the open and inviting market. Effective graphic elements retain the friendly family concept associated with Genuardi. Beautiful lighting, smart product adjacencies, consultant service and delightful displays fill the space and highlight the featured items.

The Italian Market combines textures and colors associated with neighborhood stores and open air markets; striped canvas awnings, rusting wood slatted walls, hanging salamis, cheeses and strings of garlic, woven baskets, barrels and such. The free standing floor units, in front of the L-shaped counter, tie in the old country look: stained rough pine wood accented with stacked wicker baskets. To make this area a complete shopping stop, breads and produce from other parts of the market are also shown here along with the self serve olive and pasta bar, the made-to-order calzones and the gourmet pizza station.

Italian Market

Genuardi's Family Market,
Langhorne, PA

DESIGN   *Design Forum, Dayton, OH*

GRAPHICS   *Programmed Products*

Duso's

Lonsdale Quay, W. Vancouver, BC Canada

PHOTOGRAPHER *MMP/RVC*

Typical of the shops and stands that fill the open market in the center of this festival building is Duso's Italian Market which is located prominently in the atrium and dominates by sheer size and the strong graphics. It also dominates in the variety of products displayed. Here the shopper can select from pastas, cheeses, salamis, sausages, sauces and such to prepared foods, ready-to-go especially for the many commuters who pass through on their way in and out of Vancouver via the ferry that stops in the Quay.

The Italian colors—red, white and green—are prominently displayed and then integrated into the space and the props and textures used to further the image of an open market in a village in Italy. Triangular tents of red and white canvas shield the shoppers from the sunlight that filters into the hall and they also allow

the red metal shaded incandescent lamps to work their warm and glowing magic on the assembled fruits, vegetables, meats and salads. Though this "store" is out in the open, the simple layout is self enveloping and manages to create a distinct feeling and ambiance that is specifically Duso's.

Cucina Rustica

Columbus Ave., New York, NY

DESIGN   *Nick & Patricia Rebraca, owners*

PHOTOGRAPHER   *MMP/RVC*

Cucina Rustica is a neighborhood store that is much more than it first appears to be. The prolific presentation of packaged delicacies in the turquoise painted storefront is the first indication that something special is going on here. This long, narrow and very high ceilinged store is only one door down from a charming little restaurant that is also owned and operated by the Rebracas. For some this collection of food could be considered cliche or kitsch except one has to see the love and care that goes into the exquisite presentation of prepared foods, salads, breads and condiments—all squeezed into every available inch of space in this old store. Antiques and artifacts—related and unrelated— all share the cramped space with the weathered wood counters, the "antiqued" fixtures, peasant tables and the wicker baskets that usurp most of the little aisle space that is left.

The "stained and aged" walls are overwhelmed with portraits of family from "the old country" and all is done in a witty way to appeal to the upscale and sophisticated food shoppers on Columbus Ave. They recognize the array of prepared foods presented with wild abandon and the abundance of gourmet delights and they relish their visits to this shop as much as the take-home entrees and salads they came for.

In a space of 2000 sq. ft. the design team of Bogdanow Partners Architects attempted to recreate the excitement, the sights and smells of a "timeless and authentic" noodle house/grocery/tea room on Greene St. in New York City. Like Hong Kong, the streets here are also "urban, dense and slightly industrial" and upon entering the 90 ft. long space, the store's design combines old and new elements in "elegant, unexpected ways" and the shop looks like it has always been here.

The narrow storefront windows cast light onto the tea selections, housewares and the small tables up front, while the grocery and food service area takes up the rest of the space. Sky-lit dining tables are in the very rear of the shop under the 16 ft. ceiling. The wood cases on the walls in which the teas and groceries are stocked give off a rich and warm feeling while "stark, unadorned light bulbs and a front wall left untreated (having gone many years without being touched by a paintbrush) are startling but feel very contextual." The red floor paint seems to be fading to green but the new counter tops are fresh and clean.

"The design style and variety of materials is eclectic like the functions of the space itself, and very much like the cross section of its New York customers—or for that matter—the people of Hong Kong." A truly unique shopping experience for shoppers desiring the taste of the Orient in a setting that feels Asian.

Kelley & Ping

Greene St., New York, NY

DESIGN *Bogdanow Partners, Architects, P.C.,*
New York, NY
Larry Bogdanow & Warren Ashworth

PHOTOGRAPHER *Ross Muir, New York, NY*

Bee Chang Hian

Singapore

PHOTOGRAPHER *MMP/RVC*

This project is included because it shows the importance of visual merchandising and display in food retailing. It also points up how effective lighting can sell the merchandise while creating an inviting ambiance.

Bee Cheng Hiang's grocery is located on a busy thoroughfare in Singapore across the street from the Parco—an upscale open mall created out of renovated and rehabbed 19th century chop houses. The grocery is also only a few feet away from a street-long native market of stands and stalls strung together by bare bulbs stretched out on exposed wires and an array of canvas coverings. This is where the locals shop for food, fresh fruit and vegetables, CDs, tapes, tee shirts and shorts. It is a mish-mash of mixed up merchandise presented in a typical bazaar setting yet serene and sublime, the clean and uncluttered Chinese grocery attracts and appeals to the same customer.

Specialty Food Store Design

The store's front is open to the shoppers on the street. No barrier keeps the shopper out and everything is on display. The entry floor is covered with a checkerboard of soft neutral colors and the balance of the sales floor is laid with off-white tiles. All the counters, floor units, platforms and risers as well as the shelved wall units are made of a light native wood. Live plants are everywhere adding to the good Feng Shui of the store.

The lighting is bright and clear, yet warm and flattering to the assorted fresh and prepared foods and the packaged and bottled ones on the shelves. Ceiling grids help to lower the ceiling height and created a more human scale to the space. To furthur the store's ethnic look, Chinese architectural and decorative elements are added such as the pagoda-like tile cornice over the wall shelves.

Back-lit photographs create a valance over the prepared foods counter and not only explain what is available but draw shoppers to this area. Structural columns, located throughtout the meandering space, are clad with the same wood used for the floor fixtures and they are capped with flower boxes filled with greenery and uplights. Neat, orderly, warm and inviting, well-lit and merchandised, a pleasure to shop or just behold!

La Boqueria

Las Ramblas, Barcelona, Spain

PHOTOGRAPHER *MMP/RVC*

Las Ramblas is the tree shaped walking street in the Old Gothic quarter of Barcelona. Though it is a major thoroughfare divided by a paved strip filled with strollers, sidewalk salespeople, flower stands and bird vendors, mimes and musicans, the houses on either side stand as a tribute to the art and architecture of the late 19th century.

La Boqueria is an art-nouveau inspired indoor marketplace that opens on to Las Ramblas. For almost a century it has been the main shopping center for the locals seeking produce, fish, meat, spices and farm fresh dairy products. Under the high glass and iron framework there are hundreds of stands and "shops" illuminated and signed, selling the freshest of the fresh. It is a farmers' market and a peoples' market Barcelona style.

Each stand is a specialty store: each salesperson is a specialist. They are selling knowledge as well as product. Some of the stands have been served by generations of the same family and thus the family's "name" and "integrity" are part of the product presentation.

From the point of presentation and display these stands are outstanding. There is pride of product in the care and arrangement of the merchandise and the surrounding colors and textures enhance the product. Many European cities have their own open market days and some still have their enclosed structures like La Boqueria—but these century-old buildings are disappearing as supermarkets and hypermarkets move in. When they do, it seems, they try to emulate the character of the old markets they have replaced. Yet there will always be those shoppers who would rather deal with the security and comfort of the past and buy directly from the farmers.

Gelson's Market

Northridge, CA

DESIGN *King Design International, Eugene, OR*

MARKETING & DESIGN TEAM *Becky Phegley, Michael Hopper, Chris Studach, David Thigpen*

ARCHITECT *Nadel Architects, Los Angeles, CA*

The established, upscaled chain of Gelson Food Stores added another jewel to their crown with the Northridge store. The company is known for its dedication to individuality and thus each Gelson looks and feels different from the others.

Based on the old Tuscany style architecture of the exterior, King Design International was invited to create an "Italian extravaganza" that would delight the shoppers. The inspiration came from the client: "with a theatrical flourish he cut us loose to create an interior his customers would want to write home about."

The space is filled with trees to simulate the Tuscany landscape. To create the warmth and texture of the sources of inspiration, the concrete floors are stamped to simulate streets paved with river rock and the use of the fireplaces recalls the "hearth and home" of the friendly farmers of Tuscany.

Terra cotta tiles frame shadow boxes in the stucco textured walls as well as the murals that abound in the carefully-illuminated interior. The signage and the oversized props all add to the festive spirit of Gelson's Market. Flowering vines entwine the rough textured walls and columns to further bring out of doors indoors where the shopper can stop for coffee at the cafe or buy take-out, gourmet prepared food or meals.

Puget Consumers Co-op PCC

Seattle, WA

DESIGN   *NBBJ, Seattle, WA*

DESIGN TEAM   *James Adams, Rick Buckley, Jennifer Mann, Craig Hardman, George Ostrow*

PHOTOGRAPHER   *Paul Warchol*

PCC is the nation's largest cooperatively owned national food grocer. It was established 40 years ago and this new, 13,000 sq. ft. prototype was designed by NBBJ of Seattle to "address the needs and desires of PCC's current and future customers while maintaining the allegiance of its original and founding members."

The imagery of the roadside stands, urban produce stands, gourmet kitchens and European outdoor market places provided the inspiration for the exterior and interior design. The signage on the facade recalls roadside stands while inside the produce area takes on the feeling of a European village square on market day with "small specialty shops" lining the sides of the "square."

According to George Ostrow, architect with NBBJ, "The store is designed as an urban kitchen. It is intended as an alternative to the traditional supermarket." The front of the building recalls a warehouse and the large rooftop billboard features a field of swaying wheat and emphasizes the store's natural foods. The hand painted images were painted on the perforated aluminum panels.

Inside, the produce area is the heart of the marketplace and the preparation area is in its center and the staff can interact directly with the customers. A demon54 stration kitchen teams up with the bountiful delicatessen to offer shoppers nutrition education and samples of healthy gourmet foods. In keeping with PCC's concern for the ecology, the kitchen uses non-toxic, sustainable building materials. PCC sought to reduce toxic emissions in the finished room and used recycled or all-natural materials.

The use of linoleum flooring and reclaimed douglas fir stairs did increase the building costs but these materials "add beauty to the room beyond their sustainable benefits." Custom lighting, custom fixturing, stained concrete floors and creative signing and graphics combine to create a unique and memorable urban food shopping experience.

Lebanon Co-op Food Store

Lebanon, NH

ARCHITECT *Arrowstreet, Inc., Somerville, MA*

DESIGN TEAM *Jim Batchelor, Fred Warren, John Weglarz, Amy Mackrell*

PHOTOGRAPHER *Robert K. Mikrut, Myrtle Beach, SC*

The 55,000 sq. ft. Lebanon Co-op is the heart of the new village shopping center near Dartmouth College. The challenge was not only to design a market that would meet the community's growing needs but also serve as a community gathering place and a model for environmentally friendly design.

Arrowstreet, Inc., the Somerville, MA based architects/designers, sought to evoke the image of a 19th century New England farm village and create a sense of community. The building mass is punctuated by a Shaker-inspired cupola and the building is surrounded by groves of trees and rolling hills. The building materials were chosen to minimize harm to the environment and wherever possible, recycled or benign materials were used. These materials include recycled wood trusses, concrete, steel stud framing, fiberglass insulation, countertops, carpeting and even some of the tiles. The metal roofing system was made of zinc which is durable, recyclable and produced through an environmentally friendly process.

Inside the market, natural light is used to save energy and make the shopping experience more pleasant. Dramatic light streaming down from the octagonal cupola lights up an area of special products. A soft, natural palette of green, tan and white is combined with light natural wood millwork to further add warmth to the retail setting. A counterpoint to the industrial metal ceiling are the exposed wooden trusses in the ceiling.

Much of the signage consists of blackboards framed in the light wood and they carry hand drawn "specials" in chalk as well as the permanent departmental and directional information. "The informality of the signs coordinates the Co-op's image and provides the kind of flexibility and reusability that the market values." The open spaces of the skylights and the tree-like structure of the post trusses also reinforce the connection between the inside of the market and the outside environment.

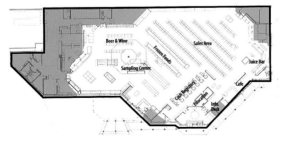

Valencia Fine Foods

Toronto, ON, Canada

DESIGN *de Signum, Toronto*

The challenge to the design firm, de Signum, was to create a warm and friendly neighborhood market where people could meet, shop and just relax.

Working within a tight budget and appealing to a multi-cultural market, the design firm relied heavily on props and decoratives to achieve the desired effect. Grain sacks, barrels, crates and antique-like elements helped to create the warm and friendly ambience without upscaling the store to a degree that it might turn off some of the desired clientele.

Warm colors, wood fixturing and brick accents are highlighted by the sharp colors used on the large graphics applied over the bakery and deli areas. The same kind of artistic whimsy appears on the store's exterior as "eye catching" graphics.

Shown here are additional views of Valencia Market. The use of simple, farm-type props and rustic textures enhance the country/casual feeling of the market.

Fruit & Co.

Pesaro, Italy

DESIGN   *Design Studio Auguzzi, Ancona, Italy*

ART DIRECTION   *Acanto, Pesaro*

MANUFACTURER   *Sifa/Sinthesi, Hollywood, FL*

PHOTOGRAPHER   *Studio 33, Pesaro*

Designed by the Design Studio Auguzzi for the Sifa/Sinthesi fixture manufacturing company to showcase their line of wall and floor systems. Fruit & Co. not only has the warmth and charm one associates with fresh fruits and produce but also sparkles with contemporary smart styling.

The fixtures of wood, painted metal and epoxide have shelves with PVC finished staves that resemble the wood. The wall shelving system allows merchandise to be presented at assorted heights while the floor units, on casters, have reclining shelves ideal for positioning fruits and vegetables. The natural beech wood (or walnut) look of the floor fixtures with their softly rounded edges are accented with a fresh spring green color that is also used on the angled wall shelves. The wall system, in this design, has a sunny yellow panel backing up the "wood" shelves and counters. Light valances, finished either in green or in wood, shield shoppers from the lights that bring color and sparkle to the produce display.

Vinyl floors simulate aged timber and the walls are finished in a warm toast color. The ceiling consists of faux beams stretched across the space with a woven matting draped over the beams. Fluorescent light fixtures, applied to the ceiling and hidden by the matting, provide a soft ambient light that filters through the bamboo matting.

Budgens, Ltd.

Midhurst, W. Sussex, England

DESIGN *John Herbert Partnership, London, England*

The 8.2000 sq. ft. market designed by the John Herbert Partnership attempts to deliver the corporate image of "Fresh, Friendly Value." The sense of openness and freshness is achieved by the use of wider aisles, lower gondola units, a green and white perimeter frieze and large scale product photographs mounted above the frieze and lit by recessed asymmetrical fixtures. The floors are finished with specially-designed terrazzo.

To enhance the feeling of a friendly local store, the customer service desk is located at the entrance. From here the shopper enters the double width produce aisle where the fixtures are low, have smartly curved ends and the light boxes above reinforce the "freshness" image.

Specialty areas were developed and given extra emphasis: the delicatessen, bakery, produce and wine shop. The delicatessen and patisserie form an end feature to the first aisle and the walls are finished with white tiles trimmed with granite. The wine department, in burgundy red and wood, is fitted with a system which allows a series of uprights to be introduced at the front of the shelves which hold regional wine signage and notification of special promotions.

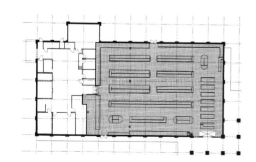

The designers treated signage as part of their overall design strategy and they developed systems for product aisle signage, special promotion ends, and aisle offers. The design team also developed a lighting plan that fits into the new metal tile ceiling.

Dearborn Sausage Co.

Detroit, MI

DESIGN *DFI, Design Fabrication Inc., Troy, MI*

PHOTOGRAPHER *Bob Montgomery, Troy, MI*

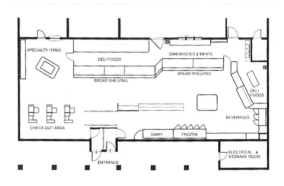

For over 50 years the Dearborn Sausage Co. has been a Michigan tradition. This family owned firm has provided kielbasa, fresh Polish sausages, spiral hams, and hot dogs to the community at large. The new 4,000 sq. ft. retail store has allowed the company to expand its product offer to include meats, delicatessen products, prepared salads and even a sandwich service counter.

The floor plan was designed to expose shoppers to the new sandwich and fresh meat areas before they reach the traditional best sellers in the delicatessen counter. To establish the traffic pattern, partial height gondolas were used so that the customers could still see into the other areas.

With "A Taste of Tradition" as the store's theme, the interior design palette reinforces the traditional look with mahogany stained oak wainscot, oak and brass fans whirring overhead, antique reproduction light fixtures suspended from the ceiling and a color scheme of navy, green and warm whites "to create an atmosphere that evokes a sense of yesteryear." As an added dollop of historic flavor, sepia-colored photographs, both old and new, decorate the walls.

A soffit drops over the service counters to draw attention to the service departments: The Dearborn Brand Delicatessen, The Butcher Shop, and The Sandwich Shop. To further emphasize these areas there are striped canvas awnings, hanging graphics, and a graphic band above the awnings featuring the spices used in making the sausages.

"The result is an interior decor that captures the old world craftsmanship and quality of the company in a retail setting."

Charcuterie Francais

Market St., Philadelphia, PA

DESIGN *Hugh Boyd Assoc., Montclair, NJ*

Located in the 30th St. Station of the Pennsylvania RR is this handsome Charcuterie designed to solve "what's for dinner?" questions for the harried and hurried commuters. Run by Rebecca Pauvert and her chef husband Marc, the shop specializes mainly in prepared foods-to-go plus some packaged items. In addition, healthful salads and entrees are on display in the white tiled space accented with mahogany.

The floor is tiled in a checkerboard of gray and white and a sunny Tuscan yellow color makes a wide swath over the white tiles. The 12 ft. long, mahogany fronted cases, shaped into an "L," are highlighted with bands of red. The floor fixtures are a mix of industrial stainless steel racks and wicker and rattan baskets and crates and bushels. Gilded frames, on the walls, list the changing menu items.

The store also does a strong boxed lunch business and relies heavily on the impulse sales of its baked goods. Napoleons are kept on display because "their eye appeal increases sales." The success of the Charcuterie has led to a "showcase" presentation as part of the Ardmore Farmers Market.

Made in Washington

Westlake Shopping Center,
Seattle, WA

DESIGN   *The Retail Group, Seattle, WA*

PRINCIPAL   *J'Amy Owens*

CEO   *Christopher Gunter, AIA*

PROJECT MANAGER   *Susan Harrison*

PHOTOGRAPHER   *Gina Hilton*

There are six Made in Washington retail stores located in the state of Washington but their proprietary specialty seafood brand of smoked salmons was not being adequately merchandised as the "star of the show" in their stores. In an effort to rectify this problem and also create a more effective presence in mall and tourist-oriented locations, The Retail Group of Seattle was invited to create a new retail setting including new fixtures to highlights the Made in Washington smoked salmon product.

The design firm created a more "northwest" feeling for the store by the use of native woods and organic looking materials and textures. The custom fixtures house each different type of salmon and highlight their products as the client requested. The shelves are angled for optimum shoppability and the face-out merchandising is visually impactful.

In addition to the salmon, the small store also stocks other products indigenous to the northwest including condiments, confectionery and hand-made souvenirs all displayed under the warm spotlights located in the blacked-out ceiling.

Jordan's Lobster Farm

Island Park, NY

DESIGN *James A. Prisco, R.A., Freeport, NY*

PHOTOGRAPHER *Tony Lopez, East End Studios, Miller Place, NY and James Prisco*

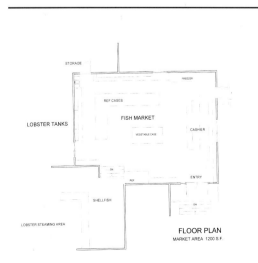

STORAGE

FREEZER

REF. CASES

FISH MARKET

LOBSTER TANKS

VEGETABLE CASE

CASHIER

ON

SHELLFISH

REF

ENTRY

ON

LOBSTER STEAMING AREA

FLOOR PLAN
MARKET AREA 1200 S.F.

The challenge to the architect James Prisco was to take what was a leaky old warehouse that had served as a lobster farm on the south shore of Long Island and convert it into an upscale sea food market reminiscent of those found on picturesque New England fishing piers.

A gabled open ceiling soars over the fish sales area. On the built-in, weathered white washed oak shelves the small colorful condiment items used in the preparation of fish and shellfish are displayed. "In a way, their repetitiousness and color contribution offer a special rhythm and style." Rounded, fish-scale shaped cedar shakes, hand painted to look weathered, are in the gable areas and the accent navy blue moldings give the space that faded, old fishing village feeling. Brushed stainless steel custom trim is used on the backsplash and also carried throughout the store and incorporated within the colorful tiled areas as an accent.

"We tried to use natural, bright colors of the raw vegetables and cooked shellfish as our palette so the paint colors are subdued and complementary." The base color of the store is a warm Irish cream accented with navy, Ming red, oyster gray and white. Salt and pepper colored granite tops cover the service counters and the vegetable market bin area. Tug boat lights are mounted behind the counter as decorative elements while low voltage halogen lights illuminate the sales area.

Lobster House

Chelsea Market, New York, NY

PHOTOGRAPHER *MMP/RVC*

Echoing the old industrial brick/concrete setting of the Chelsea Market is the Lobster House which is open for retail and wholesale sales. There is a kind of undecorated charm about the store with its easy-to-mop concrete floors, brick and concrete walls and the rough exposed structural columns that are part of the original building. A bold, almost childishly naive, mural covers one wall and adds the only explosion of color—except for the fish and shellfish—in this otherwise neutral, industrial setting.

The refrigerated cases are faced with weathered timber and the fish and shellfish—swaddled in chipped ice—are illuminated by simple fluorescent fixtures hanging over the open cases. Mostly for ambiance are the nautically inspired pendant lights in their metal cages.

As part of the ongoing "entertainment" and the enticement into the shop are the rubber aproned men in the open rear of the store, weighing, measuring, sorting and packing the live lobsters. Visitors are free to move throughout the space and look into the giant galvanized tanks filled with lobsters or at the freshly filleted or cut fish and the prepared foods shown in the glass covered cases up front.

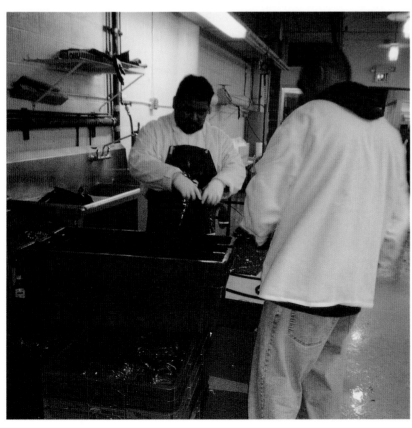

Tastefully Canadian

Vancouver International Airport,
Vancouver, BC Canada

DESIGN *Fiorino Design, Inc., Toronto, ON Canada*

GRAPHICS *Karo, Toronto, ON*

PHOTOGRAPHER *Design Archives, Toronto, ON*

FLOOR PLAN   SCALE

The design of the 650 sq. ft. space in the Vancouver Int'l Airport has to attract airport shoppers—especially visitors from Japan and other Asian countries in search of last minute "indigenous" gifts. Tastefully Canadian specializes in salmon and fish products all prepacked and prepared to travel, as well as other specialty foods and gifts such as confectionery, candy, maple syrup and maple syrup products.

Designed by Fiorino Design, Inc. of Toronto, the space planning also has to support the high volume traffic and provide for ease of merchandising and replenishment of stock by the staff. The refrigerated salmon and fish products have no "shelf appeal" so the designers expressed a fresh fish theme through the space with cherry stained maple wood, tiered fixtures, conglomerate tile flooring with green marble accents, dark green laminates on the coolers, colors of the sea, aqua and salmon colored accents and oversized, front illuminated photographs in the interior and exterior of the store.

The three dimensional exterior signage is a ribbon-like band across the open front. A refrigerated open display of fish products is up front at the lease line. It is combined with two cash/wrap stations and additional low display fixtures into a work island where customers can be served from four sides. Free standing, angled units encourage customer browsing, and the upright full service salmon cooler, freezer and full height display fixtures are set along the perimeter walls. A hand painted mural above the cooler and freezer incorporates the salmon and aqua tones of the store's design palette. An enlarged Tastefully Canadian oval graphic is incorporated within the wall fixturing.

A combination of energy efficient par lamps and low voltage halogen lamps allow for clear crisp store lighting. Accent low voltage spots are projected from the storefront bulkhead to highlight the ribbon-like sign over the entrance.

Smoked Fish Shop

Butler's Wharf, London, England

DESIGN   *CD Partnership, London, England*

Behind the stainless steel and glass storefront set into an old brick commercial building that is part of Butler's Wharf, is the Smoked Fish Shop. The minute store retails packaged smoked salmon and prepared fish dishes as well as salads, sandwiches and other foods packaged-to-go.

The all-white diagonally tiled walls are lined with white wood shelves on which condiments and packaged foods are displayed. Just under the blacked-out ceiling are a series of framed chalkboards on which menus and promotional items are chalked in.

The floor is patterned with a marbleized black and white checkerboard and the rear wall is almost completely devoted to a glass enclosed refrigerator unit. Fresh fish and shellfish are shown in a sleek black case, filled with crushed ice, that covers the entire left side of the tiny shop.

Adding a wonderful touch of color are the flowers and bouquets for sale clustered together in the center of the space under warm incandescent spots that provide the ambient as well as accent lighting for the store.

Oil & Spice Shop

Butler's Wharf, London, England

DESIGN *CD Partnership, London, England*

Located on Butler's Wharf is the Oil & Spice Shop which is most appropriate since hundreds of years ago the British East India Co. unloaded its precious spice cargoes here along the Thames.

The saffron colored interior is redolent with the aromas of the spices and herbs stored in the airtight glass containers. In addition, there is a selection of over 60 virgin olive oils and vinegars from Europe and America. Cookbooks complete this dream come true location for cooks and chefs.

The bright red and glass doors put the small space into view from the walk where visitor's to the rehabbed and restored wharf stroll. The rich yellow/gold color of the walls is complemented by the brown wood shelves that support the bottled and packaged goods. Freshly ground spices are prepacked or can be ground to order. The spices are collected in light, natural wood boxes with the names contained in brass frames on the drawer fronts.

Adding to the romance and aroma of the space are the hanging clusters of herbs and peppers. All the devices for holding and dispensing the herbs and spices are also to be found in this specialized shop: pepper mills, nutmeg graters and mortars and pestles. The Oil & Spice Shop is a "treasure trove for the accomplished cook and a happy place for those beginning their voyage of culinary discover."

This shop is part of The Gastrodome which also offers fine wines, freshly baked breads, charcuterie, cheeses, smoked fish and crustaceans (see Smoked Fish Shop).

Spice Shops

Old Spice Market, Istanbul, Turkey

PHOTOGRAPHER   *MMP/RVC*

Think spices! Think Turkey! Asia Minor! The Near and Far East! Think of places exotic, travels to unchartered destinations—think of rich aromas and the brilliant colors of saffron, cinnamon, peppers, paprika and berries and herbs.

As a classic example of a classic example, these stands in the very Old Spice Market in the centuries old, labrynth filled structure in old Istanbul are as typical as any you may see anywhere. With a vivid sense of color, the spices and herbs, lentils, olives, figs and dates are set out in crates—in bushels—in sacks or overflowing from bags for the shopper to see and to smell.

The heady aroma of the spices follow or lead the shopper, and the colors reach out and draw the shoppers towards the vivid displays. Inside the crowded shops the prepackaged foods and bottles of oils, vinegars and rose water are lined up on shelves while hanging from the ceiling is an inverted forest of dried herbs, hot hot peppers and chiles, dried mushrooms arranged in leis, garlic on strings and any other seasonings or condiments one could wish for to create the unique Turkish and near Eastern cuisine. With "art" or Artifice, the merchandise presentation demands and gets attention.

Breads · Desserts · Drinks · Midnight Snacks

Ingredients

Norwich, England

DESIGN   *Fitch, London, England*

CEO/PRESIDENT   *Jean Francois Benz*

SR. CONSULTANT   *Neil Whitehead*

PROJECT MANAGER   *Carol Dean*

PROJECT DESIGN TEAM   *Nick Butcher, Matt Merrett, Gabby Barnes, Mark Brown*

VISUAL MERCHANDISING   *John Ward*

The Don Miller Bakeries have been a High St. mainstay for many years but the company wanted to modernize their stores and set up new in-store bakery concepts for fresh baked breads. Fitch, of London, approached the design project from the "freshness" angle and from the fresh ingredients that are baked on the premises.

In the Ingredients store the baking process can be clearly seen as the bakers prepare and bake the bread. Special demonstrations reveal the latest techniques and provide new recipes. "The art of making bread and bread based products is therefore demystified and turned into theater." Customers have the option of browsing and learning about the products or simply and conveniently make their purchases. A central area displays a range of the breads and bread products from different parts of the world and samples are offered for tasting.

The vibrant ceiling colors of deep blue and red and the more subtle tints of orange and cream on the walls "create a bright energetic feel whilst still being friendly and inviting." The wording "Ingredients" runs along the walls with smaller type superimposed to highlight the particular offer. The use of graphics and color highlight and underscore the core concept: the theme of fresh ingredients and healthy products.

An area in the store is devoted to a delicatessen and juice bar. This allows for the preparation of sandwiches on breads baked in the store and the presentation of savouries, confections, jams and jellies which are also sold in the relaxing environment.

There is also a space devoted to the ingredients for baking like flour, yeast, pre-mixed dough, brown sugar, cherries and even olives that the shopper can purchase in order to recreate the taste and in-store experience at home. Freshly made pre-mixed packs also allow the Ingredients customers the ultimate combination of healthy and convenient food.

Boudin Bakery/Cafe

Berkeley, CA

DESIGN *Aumiller Youngquist, Chicago, IL*

PRINCIPAL IN CHARGE *Keith Youngquist*

PROJECT MANAGER *Nina Ricciardi*

JOB CAPTAIN *Rob Rejman*

PHOTOGRAPHER *Wolfgang Simon, La Canada, CA*

Boudin Bakeries have been a California mainstay since 1849. This family owned and operated chain—there are currently 36 stores in California, Illinois and Texas—has made its reputation based on the sourdough breads (now even bagels and pizzas) using the dough formula started by Isadore Boudin over 150 years ago. He perfected the technique of combining French baking with sourdough brought from Mexico.

The new design for a mall bakery/cafe, first introduced in Costa Mesa, is based on a 2800 sq. ft. space and seating for 40 patrons and it was designed by Aumiller Youngquit of Chicago. According to David Barrows, CEO of Boudin Bakery/Cafe, "A bakery is where you bake bread. A cafe is an experience. We've designed it to get people through, but in a comfortable, warm and visually appetizing way."

First, the shopper is aware of the wonderful aroma of the breads and the baked goods. Though the bread is baked fresh and delivered daily to each cafe/bakery, there are instore ovens for the pizzas and croissants that provide the wonderful come-on aroma. "The smell is part of the atmosphere."

As customers enter the service line they are exposed to a variety of "stations" (breads, salads, sandwiches, pizzas, and soups in edible bread "bowls"), where they have the opportunity to interact with the knowledgeable staff. If they want only breads, they can pick up their purchases and leave or they can enjoy some coffee, a snack or a light repast in a cozy yet sophisticated cafe with European touches such as tiles, faux finishes and outdoor umbrellas on the "patio."

Amy's Bread

Chelsea Market, New York, NY

DESIGN *Vandeberg Architects, New York, NY*

PHOTOGRAPHER *James Shanks & MMP/RVC*

In describing the shops and general activity in and surrounding the Chelsea Market (between 15th and 16th Sts. and 9th and 10th Aves.) in New York City, Julie V. Iovine, writing for the New York Times, described it as "a cook's cosmopolis supplying the epicure in need with everything from lobster (see Lobster House) to dairy fresh milk in a series of deli-size storefronts inside the old Nabisco factory." One of the must-see/must-try/must-buy attractions in the Chelsea Market is Amy's Bread. Here, through a series of large windows, the shopper on the brick vaulted aisle can watch breads and pastries being rolled, kneaded, formed and eventually baked. Just beyond, in a warm intimate and cozy retail store/cafe, purchases can be made to go or a patron can sit and immediately gratify his or her whetted appetite.

The long and narrow store is dominated by a wood counter that stretches along most of one of the warm, faux finished peach toned walls. The massive unit, topped with marble, is patterned with incised geometric designs. Behind it stands a black wrought iron baker's rack serving its intended purpose: filled with all sorts of wonderful fresh baked breads. The service wall, behind the counter, is partially tiled with white ceramic tiles and the area over the chair rail is mirrored. The mini-white octagonal mosaic tiled floor, accented with black, is reminiscent of the old fashioned bakeries of years and years ago. The wall opposite the long counter is all glazed and the entrance door, set amid the floor-to-ceiling high glass panels, puts the entire store on view from the aisle. On the far right wall there are some whimsical murals in artworked frames as well as more panels of mirrors. The opposite wall (left on entering) has a large window opening into the bakery beyond.

The simple tables and chairs of mahogany color and the milk glass pendant light fixtures also continue the pleasant ambience of bakery/cafe of another place and time.

Specialty Food Store Design

Saint Louis Bread

*Stratford Square Shopping
Center, Bloomingdale, IL*

DESIGN   *Marve Cooper, Lieber Cooper, Inc.,
Chicago, IL*

PRINCIPAL IN CHARGE   *Marve Cooper*

DIRECTOR OF DESIGN   *Keith Curtis*

SR. DESIGNER/PROJECT DESIGNER   *Pablo*

DESIGNER   *Maria DeLucia*

PHOTOGRAPHER   *Marc Ballogg,
Steinkamp/Ballogg, Chicago, IL*

The Saint Louis Bread Company is making its imprint in malls and shopping centers not only as a casual cafe but as a bakery where shoppers can select from a variety of freshly baked breads and baked goods—and still enjoy a coffee break during a shopping excursion.

It is the bread, the aroma and the sight of the loaves—that is the main attraction here and the overall look of the space was inspired by contemporary casual European cafes. The textures and materials "create a context from which visual stimulants are composed throughout the space."

The all-important bakery, on the premises, is the core of the design and it is defined by the large gentle arch in front of it and the red tiles. The area is "visually enriched" with overflowing bakery displays and packages of bread. The balance of the walls of the shop are washed with a soft ocher color that creates a warm, glowing background for the woods and the neutral fixtures. In contrast to the color and the old bakery/cafe feeling, the tables and chairs were selected because they are "classic contemporary" and add to the new look of the space.

The surrounding graphics like the banners, signage, and menuboards play an integral part in the design by adding "splashes of color and information" throughout the space.

Payard Patisserie

Lexington Ave., New York, NY

DESIGN *Rockwell Architects, New York, NY*

Imagine a long established neighborhood bakery/cafe on the left bank of Paris—warm, friendly and cozy. Now enter the 2700 sq. ft. space on Lexington Ave. in New York City and be surrounded by the same sights, smells and feelings.

To enhance the spacious feeling, the storefront and vestibule area were conceived in wood and marble. High ceilings and a warm creamy palette plus mahogany woodwork further emphasize the open feeling of the shop. Not only can the window shoppers enjoy the luscious displays of baked goods and desserts, but they can also see into the dining and mezzanine areas of the store. In the pastry shop, chocolates, candies, pastries, breads and packaged gifts are displayed on custom mahogany and marble cases.

Separating the pastry shop from the dining room is the sinuous coffee/liquor bar which serves the morning, afternoon tea-time and after dinner dessert crowds.

Through architectural and design details, one space flows easily into the next. An expansive plaster frieze, inspired by white pastry, and a Roman mosaic floor border embedded with illustrations of croissants, baguettes and pastries enrich the space as do the large mirrors in Belle Epoch gilt frames and the blown glass light fixtures. All together they reinforce the European cafe inspiration of the design.

L' Epicerie

Ile St. Louis, Paris, France

DESIGN *Yabu Pushelberg, PQ, Canada*

PHOTOGRAPHER *MMP/RVC*

Anybody who has ever wandered about in Paris—on the Left or Right Bank—must have at one time slowed down to enjoy the relaxed and tasteful shopping on the long but narrow Ile St. Louis which lies between the two banks of the Seine. On the long shopping street that forms the spine of the island is L' Epicerie—a delicious shop that specializes in coffee, tea, chocolate, and preserves.

The exterior facade is part of the venerable building that houses the store and it is painted a rich, deep green. The logo, in gold, appears on the fascia over the door. Inside, the small and compact store is almost totally sheathed in a tawny, mellow colored wood.

The floor is covered with small, off-white ceramic squares and the area over the high wood library wall cabinets is painted a subtly muted terra cotta color. Logos and old time advertisements for coffee, tea, and chocolate products are framed and create a decorative band around the store—over the merchandise.

The wall shelves gently step back—the deepest shelf being the lowest one—so that the merchandise on the upper shelves can be seen with gift suggestions and pre-wrapped gifts. The cash/wrap desk stands directly behind them and thus an island of merchandise in the center creates the traffic pattern.

Coffee People

Portland, OR

DESIGN *RPA, Columbus, OH*

V.P. CREATIVE DESIGN *Diane Perduk Rambo*

PHOTOGRAPHER *Christian Deuber*

The Coffee People, in an effort to "transcend demographic boundaries" and find a niche for the company, commissioned the design firm, Retail Planning Associates of Columbus, to come up with a new/old look. What evolved and is shown here is a "distinctly American Coffee House—one with a 1960s beat culture inspired ethic espousing humanistic values such as tolerance, inclusiveness and individualism." The design combines tongue-in-cheek humor with civic courtesy and responsibility, "positioning itself for a young, culturally curious and highly educated consumer."

The shop features natural wood materials, sunny yellow and carob browns "giving this particularly American palette its undeniable warmth and its retro-kitsch appeal." A kaleidosocipic array of oranges, purples, olives and blues accentuate the space. The carob brown sets off the floor graphics' accent colors, which were based on Harry Beroia lithographs,—"chosen for their organic quality and fluid content." The brown also marks off the traffic pattern with fun words such as "sing" and "dream" painted in white to lead the patron through the different areas. Above, a "psychedelic suspended ceiling" installation serves as a whimsical counterpoint to the floor pattern.

The window bar area serves the "grab-and-go" coffee drinkers while the over-stuffed chairs and side tables allow for a more leisurely enjoyment of the coffee or light repast under the swirling, colored, translucent disk suspended over this second seating area.

A third area is provided for persons who come in for a "break" before going on to the next appointment. In this area, two-top tables can be grouped as needed. Surrounding these areas are the sunny yellow/gold walls that complement the menu boards and the all-important Bean-O-Rama at the rear of the shop.

Bean-O-Rama is the retail coffee bean area and the specially designed curved cabinetry displays 24 different coffees/blends. As an extra enticement, customers are invited to spin a roulette wheel in a chance of winning free coffee. Back here it is business (and play) and patrons are not jammed up waiting for service.

In keeping with the "democratic spirit" of Coffee People, a community board is provided for customers to display items of community or personal interest.

Cup 'O' Joe

Lennox Town Center, Columbus, OH

DESIGN *Chute Gerdeman, Columbus, OH*

ACCOUNT EXECUTIVE *Denny Gerdeman*

PROJECT MANAGER *Greg DeLong*

SR. DESIGNER ENVIRONMENTAL
Maribeth Gatchalian-Mooney

DESIGNERS *Michelle Isroff & Heidi Kretzmann*

DESIGN DEVELOPMENT *Jeff Kreidler*

ARCHITECT *White Associates, Columbus, OH*

PHOTOGRAPHER *Michael Houghton,
StudiOhio, Columbus, OH*

The 1800 sq. ft. space in the Lennox Town Center as designed by the Chute Gerdeman design firm is a comfortable and intimate space with universal appeal. Everyday materials, used cleverly and surprisingly, add to the charm and the success of the overall design.

A 12 ft. diameter by six ft. tall coffee mug, perched atop the roof of the entrance, greets the potential coffee buyer/drinker. Inside, the space is divided into three featured areas: the food and ordering counter, the "living room" where the coffee can be sipped and savored and the By-The-Pound zone for the retail sales. The coffee-by-the-pound display offers the best international coffee beans while the counter patrons can select from specialty coffee drinks, tea, sandwiches and gourmet desserts. The dining room is a relaxed area with a warm and comforting fireplace that is visible from anywhere in the store. The seating options include soft seating (plus sofas and easy chairs), some circular booths and unusual wood tables with inset detailing and traditional chairs. Extremely popular—weather permitting—are the outdoor tables and chairs.

"Uncommon use of uncommon materials defines the tactile language of the space." Some of the materials used include copper tubing, screen mesh, pegboard, newspapers as wallpaper, and coffee bean panels. Used coffee cans and copper tubing make some rather decorative lighting fixtures. The cans are perforated and then branded with the Cup 'O' Joe logo. Incandescent lamps are used throughout to contrast with the blues and greens of the upholstery fabrics. The flooring varies from area to area: mottled assorted tones of brown porcelain tiles at the entrance, and the dining area mixes hardwood floors with lime green carpet insets. Black tile flooring surrounds the espresso bar. The walls are a muted ocher yellow and some areas are covered with "newspapers," graphics and tiles.

The owner, Todd Applebaum, said, "We fell in love with the whole concept of a coffee house. When people come out of college they are looking for somewhere a little more mature than a bar to hang out in. We couldn't fit it—so we created it." Thus— Cup 'O' Joe.

Pasqua Coffee Bar

San Francisco, CA

DESIGN *Grid/2 International, New York, NY*

PRESIDENT *Martin Roberts*

V.P. PROJECT MANAGER
Betty Chew & Akka Ma

DESIGN ASSOCIATE *Jeffrey Cook*

DESIGNER *Mary Ann Boyton*

ARCHITECT *Iyer & Assoc., San Francisco, CA*

PHOTOGRAPHER *Peter Paige, Harrington Park, NJ*

The Pasqua Coffee people desiring greater consumer recognition in a market that is rapidly becoming over saturated, approached Grid/2 Int'l, of New York. The company wanted a new store concept and a complete graphics program "to increase customer awareness for the Pasqua brand while conveying an impression of speedy service."

Though the majority of their customers come in during morning and lunch hours for coffee-to-go," it was the retail gourmet bean part of Pasqua that needed help.

Grid/2 Int'l developed category differential through graphic imagery and in-store presentation to stress the gourmet bean product. The new colors are "hot": Moroccan red and rich cream. The new graphic identity depicts a moving figure carrying a steaming cup of coffee and a paper bag. "In consideration of ethnic diversity, the figure is shown in relief."

The retail products—the beans and blends—are packaged in the new and enriched colored packages and they are prominently displayed in the quick-service bar. In order to inject energy into the space, which can be quite empty during the off-hours, a large wall mural dominates the relatively small space and it shows a mass of culturally diverse characters in strong and exciting colors: reds, coffee brown, cream, gray and black.

The wall behind the copper colored service bar is Moroccan red and the rest of the walls and the tiled floor are cream colored. The same light color is used on the laminate topped tables accented with a red band and for the molded plastic chairs. The rich red color is also used for the vinyl upholstery on the banquette under the mural. This design has received several trade and trade magazine awards.

The Daily Grind

Northridge, CA

DESIGN *R.W. Smith & Co.*

Karen Moncrief

PHOTOGRAPHER *Milroy/McAleer*

The retail coffee shop/cafe, The Daily Grind, opened in the newly renovated Northridge Mall in California. The objective for the designers at R.W. Smith & Co. was to provide an inviting upscale contemporary gourmet coffee store that would showcase the retail business.

The front window consists of a stainless steel cable system with glass shelves on which cookie jars and teapots are featured. Inside the store, the flamed copper wrapped structural column demands the viewer's attention. The column tops are treated with a pearlescent teal paint and accented with "ribbons" of purple metal mesh attached with brass rods to the internally-lit column. The same flamed copper appears in the back upper soffit, below which the retail coffees and teas are presented.

The floor is Forbo linoleum in large, gold mottled squares with black accent strips. The main counter has a deep purple laminate over a yellow/gold stained beech body. The unit is finished with black metal dividers and polished black and copper granite.

Koffee & Cream

Toronto, ON Canada

DESIGN *International Design Group, Toronto, ON Canada*

A Mediterranean theme was developed for this street level shop that specializes in and integrates the sales of gourmet coffees with sandwiches, pastries and ice cream. The client wanted a warm, friendly and casual setting that would attract customers for breakfast, lunch and evening snacks—as well as all day long for coffee.

The space is long and narrow: only 760 sq. ft. with a low ceiling. The designers added an atrium-like bay window to "open up the space and provide a flood of daylight." The focal point, at the entrance, is the curved counter of green marble and lacewood. It features a display of coffee sacks and a variety of fresh brewed coffees. The graphic above the bright logo echoes the curve of the counter which also introduces the gentle traffic flow towards the rear of the space. The largely off-white space is decorated with large blow-ups of graphics from coffee packaging and they are used as a stencil trim and as framed photographs.

Air conditioning ducts are concealed inside a lower stepped bulkhead on the wall behind the display cases which leaves additional height in the customers' seating area. A lower ceiling bulkhead undulates from front to rear and it is accented with neon illumination "to break the lineal feel of the space." There were pipes running vertically down the wall behind the seating area and these are enclosed in panels providing modular interest to the wall.

The dramatic use of lighting to feature the merchandise presentation, wall graphics and the table tops, all add to the intimacy, the light and warm environment and "the congenial quality of a European cafe."

Joffrey's Coffee & Tea Co.

Tampa, FL

DESIGN: *ArchitecturePlus Intl., Inc., Tampa, FL*

PROJECT EXECUTIVE *Juan F. Romero, AIA*

DESIGN DIRECTOR *Thomas Henken*

GRAPHIC DESIGN *Barbara Smithey*

PHOTOGRAPHER *George Cott, Chroma, Inc., Tampa, FL*

The prototype design for the Joffrey Coffee & Tea Co. encompasses 2400 sq. ft. The roll-outs will eventually be located in upscale neighborhoods and in entertainment centers because in addition to selling coffee and tea in bulk, the shop serves gourmet coffees, teas and desserts.

Over 50 varieties and roasts of coffee and 20 varieties of teas are offered, in bulk, through a kiosk that has been designed to make selection a simple process. It also is sequestered away from the bustle and lines waiting for coffee-by-the-cup sales. The cafe concept caters to moviegoers, after dinner dessert and coffee drinkers as well as people looking for a spot to rest and sip an espresso or a special brew.

To complement the rich color of the coffees, the designers used warm woods and marbles. Copper and bronze medallions, finials and graphics adorn the cabinetry "adding sparkle and a touch of refinement." Joffrey's signature teal color stands out from the rich neutrals and metallic accents.

To create comfortable and intimate levels of illumination in the area that can seat 60 (another 40 can be served outside) and to spotlight the product display and the graphics, halogen spots are used. They also emphasize the contrast between materials and textures.

Lipton Tea House

Pasadena, CA

DESIGN *Donovan & Green, New York, NY*

PROJECT DIRECTOR *Nancye Green*

CREATIVE DIRECTOR *Andrew Drews*

PROJECT MANAGER *Paul Soulellis*

DESIGNERS *Vanessa Ryan & John Chu*

FOR LIPTON'S TEA *Jim Reid, President*

PHOTOGRAPHER *Jim Hedrich, Hedrich Blessing Photographers, Chicago, IL*

The prototype design for the new retail store for the Thomas J. Lipton Co. was recently built and opened in Pasadena, CA. The Lipton Co. has great name recognition as the largest producer of tea in the world but the concept of a retail store to sell the many different types of packaged teas was new. Based on this design, the company plans to roll out about 200 outlets in the near future.

The palette for the Teahouse was chosen to reflect the greens of the tea plant and the golden hues of the brewed beverage. An information rail, at the front of the shop, "engages customers at counter height with images, text, and graphics of Lipton's history and tea culture in general." Light colored natural woods, colored glass and upholstered banquettes and more graphic images of tea create a soothing salon-like ambiance in the rear of the space where about three dozen patrons can be seated.

There is a dropped circular disk over the circular, two-tiered, counter up front which serves as a refreshment center as well as a sales counter. Along the two sides of the store there are wood cubicles lined with tea pots and other tea making accessories—all for sale.

A dropped, open grid of the same timber creates an intimate Asian tea house look for the seated patrons in the rear. The very high, metal covered ceiling is painted off-white and it reflects light that streams up from behind the circular ceiling disk over the counter. Focused incandescent lamps, partially hidden by a wood fascia extending out in front of the boxed-off wall units, illuminate the displayed packages and tea accessories.

Without being overdone with trite or cliche "Asian architectural details" the space still creates the look of a contemporary and sophisticated Oriental tea house.

Tea Box

Takashimaya, Fifth Ave., New York, NY

DESIGN *S. Russell Groves, New York, NY*

PHOTOGRAPHER *Peter Mauss, ESTO, New York, NY*

On the lower level of the Takashimaya Department Store on Fifth Ave. in New York City, S. Russell Groves, the New York City-based designer, was challenged to "create a light-filled and open environment" in the below grade and windowless site.

The main design element used to open the space is a series of screens made of wire brushed oak. The screens neither touch each other nor the ceiling and they serve to divide the space, visually, into a retail and a tea drinking area. "Space flows between the areas and the two programs are further articulated with textures and shade." Lighter tones line the retail area while darker ones are used to surround the dining space. A fabric ceiling softens and expands the otherwise low ceiling.

The floors are light: flame finished, bleached white oak and honed limestones. For the walls there are a variety of finishes, as noted above, which include a lacquer finish (Fresco Decorative Painting), a textured plaster wall finish (Jim Hurley Studio) and aluminum leafing (Maureen). The neutral off-white, silver, steel and oak woods all underscore the feeling of a contemporary, Oriental-inspired space.

Duty Free Shop

Millenia Mall, Singapore

DESIGNER *Charles Sparks + Co., Westchester, IL*

In Singapore where drinking of alcoholic beverages is not illegal but definitely not encouraged (the high sin taxes make drinking restrictive), the giant Duty Free Shop in the Millenia Mall does a brisk business selling wines and liquors to tourists, travelers and locals alike.

The Spirits Shop is located in the three level space which is divided into zones to facilitate shopping. The main design references used by the design firm, Charles Sparks + Co. of Westchester, IL. are the Modernists of the 1920's and 1930's. It is the elegant style that flourished in the fashion salons of Paris. They also "borrowed" from the late 19th cent.-early 20th cent. Viennese architects with their outline details and geometric order. Thus, rectangles, squares, circles and ovals work in counterpoint with each other, both in the plan of the space and in the decorative details of that space. Extensive use of revealed veneer panels is also suggestive of the wainscoting and the architraves found in the classical modern European salons.

In the Spirits area, the same open, airy and elegant sense of space and design rules supreme.

The 3550 sq. ft. space in the United Airlines Terminal of the San Francisco Airport was designed by Sunderland Innerspace Design, Inc. based in Vancouver, BC. Throughout the design there is are references to the Golden Gate Bridge. The perimeter bulkhead "mimics" the underside of the bridge deck and the wall merchandise units "replicate the 'C' channels, and the signature structural pylon dividers are articulated in the product feature displays." The store's colors also depict the bridge's colors as one might see them at sunset on an autumn day. The "blue sky" is "subliminally" represented over the centralized cash wraps and it also serves as a backdrop for the store's presentation.

Regional foods, wines and candy are among the featured items. The gradation of fixtures and displays ensures a clear line of vision through the store and to the interesting focal points within each area. "The visual displays and striking photographic images further articulate the concept integrity and enhance the quiet elegance of the store overall."

Golden Gate Connection

San Francisco Airport, San Francisco, CA

DESIGN   *Sunderland Innerspace Design, Inc., Vancouver, BC*

DESIGN TEAM   *Jon Sunderland, Jonathon McNeely, Janice McAllister*

ARCHITECT   *Joseph Chow Assoc.*

PHOTOGRAPHER   *Milroy McAleer Photography, Costa Mesa, CA*

Wine Shop

*Ambassador Duty Free Shop,
Windsor, ON Canada*

DESIGN *International Design Group, Toronto, ON*

PHOTOGRAPHER *Design Archives, Toronto*

AMBASSADOR DUTY FREE STORE

With its bright clean design and combination of natural imagery, materials and extensively fabricated fixtures, this duty free shop provides a welcoming environment for travel weary shoppers." One of the more popular areas in this DFS located in the airport in Windsor is the Wine Shop designed by International Design Group of Toronto, ON.

A self-service department store approach has been created which makes it less intimidating for shoppers to browse and unique environments have been designed for the various products: the wine area suggests an old wine cellar with suspended lighting and special wine shelves.

Sweeping curved walls envelop the area and set this shop apart from the balance of the Duty Free Shop. The maple wood wall and floor fixtures are accented with nickel and all were customized to be rearrangeable. The floor units, on casters, are set on angles to permit browsers to easily reach the perimeter wall stock displays.

The deep terra cotta colored linoleum floor adds to the "wine" concept while the sage green complements the product offering and the natural wood fixtures. Old wine barrels add to the overall ambience as do some other collected memorabilia. The lighting consists of recessed compact fluorescent accented with track lighting.

Best Cellars

New York, NY

DESIGN: *Rockwell Group, New York, NY*
David Rockwell

PHOTOGRAPHER: *Paul Warchol*

Best Cellars is a "radically new concept" in wine retailing. The owners, Joshua Wesson, Michael Green and Richard Marmet, wanted to de-mystify wine and make it a readily understood and accepted product: easy to select and fun to buy and try. The concept was to advance the idea of "wine for every day."

In the 800 sq. ft. space, the store sells 100 wines that retail for under $10. a bottle. Instead of designating the wines by grape type, wine region or country, the wines are organized by categories such as "soft," "luscious," "juicy," "sweet," and "fizzy."

A very light wood—American sycamore—surrounds the room and it is accented by the handrubbed burgundy colored plaster walls. The floors are polished concrete. Custom back-lit cabinetry display the bottles and also provide a spectrum of colors that seem to reach out to the shoppers on the street.

The Wine Cellar

Masquerade Village, Rio Suites Hotel, Las Vegas, NV

DESIGN   *Marnell/Corrao Assoc., Las Vegas, NV*

Neighboring the Napa Valley Gourmet (also in this book) on the main floor of Masquerade Village—the all day, all night festival place in the Rio Suites Hotel in Las Vegas—is an ornate wrought iron arch that leads down turning stone paved steps to the Wine Cellar. When the visitor arrives at the below grade level, it seems as though he or she is in a time warp.

It is a place that seems to have been there for centuries. The ceiling consists of vaults and arches outlined with massive bricks and some walls are stuccoed and finished in a warm beige. Piers and supporting walls are constructed of cut and fitted field stone while the floors are paved with hand made tiles in various shades of terra cotta and brown.

The passageways, alleyways, nooks, crannies and cul-de-sacs of the Wine Cellar are delineated by bands of brickwork set into the tile flooring. Service counters, wine racks, and wall storage units are constructed of rich red/orange stained wood which all adds to the warm and cozy ambiance of the low lit, low ceilinged space. Wine barrels are used to feature promotional items in front of the stone covered piers and "ancient" candelabra and torcheres of black wrought iron, con-

tribute interest and texture to the space. Long simple rectory tables, with chairs around them, are used for the wine tasting sessions that are so popular here.

The Wine Cellar "brings together the world's largest and most extensive collection of fine and rare wines" that run the gamut from wines produced in the Bordeaux region of France to those from Napa Valley in California. There are at least 32,000 bottles in stock in this wine shop at any time. In addition, there is the wine tasting room merchandise that includes signature glassware, logo apparel, decanters, stoppers, corkscrews and gift certificates.

LCBO Manulife

Manulife Centre, Toronto, ON
Canada

DESIGN *Fiorino Design Inc., Toronto, ON*

GRAPHIC DESIGN *Heather Cooper*

PHOTOGRAPHER *Design Archives, Toronto, ON*

The challenge presented to Fiorino Design Inc. of Toronto was twofold. First, they had to expand the existing wine/spirit store to 5500 sq. ft. and, since market research indicated that Manulife Centre's shoppers were 55% women, the space was to be upgraded to reflect the customer's interest. They were to create a "dynamic shopping environment" that would be "welcoming and non-intimidating and appeal equally to men and women customers."

The designers emphasized the romantic and natural origins of the products by means of color, texture, and art that are traditional to wine producing. The store's layout encourages exploration and browsing and a kitchen/demonstration area draws shoppers to the rear of the space. There is a circular information center up front and the cash desks fan out to one side of the entrance.

The color palette is warm and inviting—"relaxed yet stimulating": a sunny court-yard atmosphere created with yellow/cream stuccos, curved perimeter walls. The illusion is furthered by the sand and terra cotta two-toned linoleum that emu-lates gravel. Ochers, gray-greens and ivory complete the color scheme. Specialty areas are housed within stucco framed archways flanked by overscale "impres-sionistic" paintings. The beer area is designed, in contrast, to be crisp, clean and refreshing. Vertical half barrels are used as fixtures for pre-packed beer. The local wine section has ocher lacquered wall fixturing with a traditional cornice.

The fixtures are mainly natural, quarter cut maple with cream laminate shelves. In addition, round, tiered gray metal tables with sandblasted tops hold featured promotional wines and the tables add to the desired outdoor garden look. That imagery is also captured in the topiary-like sandblasted metal tiered display fix-tures with gray/green planter box bases.

The lighting is a combination of energy saving, recessed compact fluorescent and par lamps with perimeter low voltage halogens contributing to the sunny, out-of-doors ambiance.

LCBO Image

Avenue Road, Toronto, ON Canada

DESIGN   *Fiorino Design, Inc., Toronto, ON*

PROJECT AND DESIGN COORDINATOR
Kneider Architects, Toronto, ON

GRAPHIC DESIGN   *Heather Cooper*

PHOTOGRAPHER   *Design Archives, Toronto, ON*

Based on the success of the Manulife design, Fiorino Design was asked to rework its typical roll out design and translate the plan so that it was focused more on customer service in the lighter, romantic "courtyard" atmosphere.

This new plan not only addresses the exterior of the store but places service front and center with angled checkouts in the background. Featured is a diagonal "power aisle" that draws shoppers to the "Vintages" area where there are new end-aisle POP chalkboard displays and a trompe l'oeil and T-bar ceiling treatment. The layout "weaves" shoppers through the store and also encourages browsing and exploration.

The interior color scheme is sage green, cream, white and natural pearwood colored maple. The floors are also paved with the gravel-like sand and terra cotta colored linoleum. The gift center has sage lacquered wall fixturing with traditional cornice detailing and ocher pinstripe accents. All gondolas and perimeter metal shelving are cream epoxy paint finish with natural maple moldings and signage/canopy treatments. The signage has been re-proportioned and lowered to allow for better sight lines. Perimeter canopy signage has traditional cornice detailing.

The wine cellar look of the "Vintages" area has open cubes of pearwood colored maple with screen mesh upper cabinet doors. In addition, back illuminated column details in natural maple with sage green accents plus the hand painted wall graphics help to set this special section apart from the "sunny courtyard" look of the rest of the space.

LCBO Image
Avenue Road, Toronto, ON

LCBO Queen St.

Queen St., Toronto, ON Canada

DESIGN *International Design Group, Toronto, ON*

PHOTOGRAPHER *Design Archives, Toronto*

This 1200 "mini" shop on Queen St. caters to the modern urban shopper yet the store's overall aura alludes to an abstracted rural vineyard with stylized grapevines, arbors and pergolas. The "specialty store" atmosphere of the shop bolsters the image of the Liquor Control Board of Ontario image as a progressive and consumer oriented purveyor of quality wines, spirits and beers.

The glazed two-story storefront attracts attention from the street with the 20 ft. x 12 ft. high mural by Antonio Cangesni that is featured directly inside the store. This store, which stocks approximately 600 brands of wine/liquor/beer, is long and only 19 ft. wide. To minimize the "bowling ally" feeling, the length is broken down by tall showcases that line both sides of the store and the striped floor pattern that draws attention to the crossways.

Distinct and cost effective materials were used to "express the individuality of the store while maintaining a cohesive and harmonious whole." High gloss, medium density fiberboard complements the natural beech wood and both are contrasted by the natural pewter finish of the wrought iron work that is entwined on the floating wood ceiling grid that punctuates the sales and service counter as well as the organic wrought iron detailing on the wall fixtures. The bold floor pattern is a natural linoleum sheet that is resilient underfoot. It contrasts with the hardness of the woods and the bottles. A natural slate and recessed drainage mat is offset from the regular floor pattern and serves as a practical flooring for street traffic.

"The generous ceiling height and bold architectural nature of the space combined with indigenous materials and attention to detail creates an impressive background that reinforces the quality of the merchandise and the shopping experience.

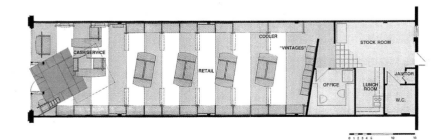

LCBO Market Village

Toronto, ON Canada

DESIGN *International Design Group, Toronto, ON*

PHOTOGRAPHER *Design Archives, Toronto*

This small (only 650 sq. ft.) shop is targeted at the Hong Kong/Chinese immigrants who live in the greater Toronto area. Targeted especially are the affluent shoppers to whom spirits are a status symbol and also ideal gifts for business and entertaining.

The boutique, designed by Toronto-based International Design Group, is designed with an international flavor that alludes to an Eastern influence. The corner entry is framed by majestic pedimented columns and the Asian portal sets the mood for the store's simple but bold atmosphere. The Asian ambiance is further implied by the vibrant palette of mahogany stained cherry, eggplant purple, spring green and pale yellow.

The principles of Feng Shui were followed with regard to placement, location and the use of colors. A sweeping wall of "Mondrian-like" cubicles frame the products and provide flexibility for a broad product assortment. The focal point of the store is the consultation/service/greeting area which is reinforced by a suspended ceiling.

The elliptical cut in the linoleum floor mirrors the dropped ceiling design. Immediately behind this desk is the Cognac area. For special tasting events, the guest chairs and consultation table can be moved and the omission of floor fixtures allows for comfortable, unobstructed movement especially at high traffic times.

"The simplicity of the plan, subtle detailing and clean lines give the store a Tao-like atmosphere and contribute to the refined elegance" The store's ambiance, knowledgeable staff and special taste testing events appeal to the sophisticated tastes and needs of the chosen market.

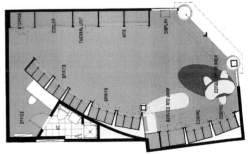

The Wine Shop

Butler's Wharf, London, England

DESIGN   *CD Partnership, London, England*

Located in the new fun and "in" place to go—Butler's Wharf—is the Gastrodome which features The Wine Shop. The Wharf is in an old, and for some time neglected, area that is being rehabbed and revitalized with shops, restaurants and even smart apartments for Londoners to reside in. Along with the Oil & Spice Shop and the Smoked Fish Shop, also in this edition, is this long, narrow wine and spirits shop.

The gently vaulted ceiling is covered with long, thin strips of timber that enhance the enclosed tunnel-like space, as well as suggest part of a giant wine keg. The long perimeter walls are lined with shelves from floor to the arced ceiling and the wood has been stained a mahogany color. Up to, about six ft from the floor, the shelves are angled so that the bottle labels can be read and on the upper shelves the bottles are lined up vertically.

The walls are painted a warm gray and the concrete floor is stained and scored and occasionally accented with areas of wood planking. A large rustic rectory table and chairs is set in the center of the space under the row of incandescent spots that line the wood ceiling. It is here that wine tasting and consultations are done. No floor fixtures are used but featured "arrivals" or "specials" are piled up in the open wood crates for shoppers to peruse.

The brick lined arched doorway into the shop echoes the vaulted ceiling. The tripart door is highlighted with panels of red, yellow and blue glass.

Vintages

Hazelton Lanes, Toronto, ON
Canada

DESIGN *International Design Group, Toronto, ON*

PHOTOGRAPHER *Design Archives, Toronto*

Vintages is one of the anchor tenants in the sophisticated upscale, two level Hazelton Lanes in Toronto, ON. Though the store is in the center court of the mall, the view of the storefront is somewhat impacted by the escalators. To overcome this handicap, the architects/designers extended the lease line under the escalator space to affect an arcade look in the first ten feet of the space. They continued the mall finishes and materials through the arcade and the impression is that it is a natural extension and the escalator is part of Vintages store design.

A low key cellar concept was selected with emphasis on wine tasting and consumer information. The physical environment was to be tasteful and inviting and correspond to the high standards of the mall.

To reinforce the cellar concept, brick was used extensively on all columns and formed arches. Ceilings are an open mesh grid system with low voltage halogen lamps above the grid. Throughout, the floor is laid in a diagonal plaid which is a combination of natural stone and marble and it is similar to the floors of the mall's aisles. All the fixtures are constructed of clear lacquered white birch trimmed with brass wine holders.

Neon was used on all major signs inside and outside the store "to enhance the traditional logo created specifically for this concept."

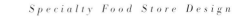

Bottle Your Own

Crossroads Mall, Toronto, ON Canada

DESIGN   *International Design Group, Toronto, ON*

PHOTOGRAPHER   *Design Archives, Toronto*

The bulk aisle concept of your favorite supermarket has just moved into the local wine/spirit shop. This new pilot project of the Liquor Control Board of Ontario offers its customers a bulk format for greater value. Customers are invited to bring their own bottles to fill from the large casks but not before they have had the opportunity to taste the high quality Canadian, Californian and Chilean red and white wines being featured.

Because a large space is needed to properly conduct a bulk format operation, this space of 7000 sq. ft., in a power center, was selected. The targeted market consists of younger customers looking for value and who enjoy the do-it-yourself experience. It also appeals to ethnic shoppers who are accustomed to bulk shopping as well as middle-to-higher income customers who enjoy wine but want an inexpensive house brand. To make the space work, it required a spacious, well organized layout and easily recognized stations.

For first-time patrons, the Ask Us station, up front, provides guidance and direction on how things are done. The next step, logically, is the Tasting station to sample the featured wines. Since customers are encouraged to "recycle" their wine bottles, a Rinse station allows for getting the bottles ready to be filled, corked and labeled.

Each station is treated as a separate design with durable colors and materials selected to reinforce the station's purpose. The Rinse area features porcelain tile walls and clear lacquer MDF boards. Cork floor tiles are used to line the walls in the Corking station and the Bottle Your Own station has a bright orange dropped ceiling that draws attention to this location. Most of the vast space is painted a subtle shade of LCBO's corporate green.

Colorful bulkheads of assorted shapes and sizes add a visual element to the store as they mask the high ceiling. The 16 ft. mural of red and white grapes makes a dynamic visual presence in the store. There is an elegant display area marked Events which informs shoppers of the products featured in the traditional LCBO shop located next door.

As bulk shopping produces wear and tear, durable materials and finishes were used like MDF board for the fixtures and sealed concrete floors. "Warm colors, light materials, bulkheads and murals combat the sterile, cold feel of the customer area to create a friendly, welcoming environment."

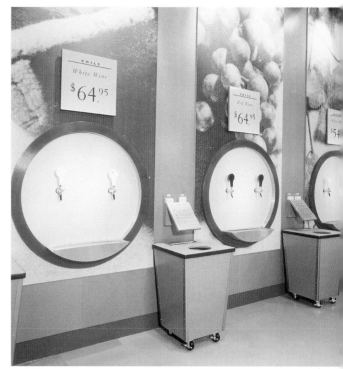

The French Wine Merchant

The Source, Westbury, NY

DESIGN   *Weisberg-Castro Association, NY*

PHOTOGRAPHER   *Ron Glassman, NY*

Maurice Amiel, known as the French Wine Merchant to his many clients in Manhattan, now has lent his title to this handsome shop at The Source, a new mall in Westbury, NY. "We have the space of a mega-store with the feel of a wine gourmet's specialty shop offering daily wine tastings, wine education classes and a wide selection of gift and holiday baskets." This is all in addition to the extensive stock of French, Italian, Spanish, Australian, California, Organic and Kosher wines.

Dramatizing the large space are the slatted wood vaulted ceilings hanging over the space that suggest giant wine kegs. The recurring arch motif is repeated on the black, horizontally paneled wood wall. The balance of the perimeter walls are a rich, wine flavored burgundy color that is also used for the stained and polished floor. Wines are lined up on shelves on the walls under graphics and display shadow boxes that help to explain the origin or final use of the wines.

Specially designed gondolas that look more like skeletal shipping crates are lined up on the floor and each one is finished with arrow shaped end panels that carry signage designating the place of origin of the assembled wines. The uppermost shelf of each gondola is angled—like the arrow head—so that the wine bottles are readily seen and the labels easily read.

The lighting is low keyed and dramatic but still efficient for shopping and reading the fine print on the labels. In addition to the low voltage halogen lamps suspended down from the curved wood ceilings, there are half round up-lights highlighting some areas and the hidden lights accentuate the graphics and displays over the shelves on the walls.

In addition, in a wine lover's boutique, there are many different accessories like openers, stoppers, wine racks and books. This store also boasts of the only temperature controlled rooms for auction house quality wines on Long Island as well as refrigerators for some of the "chilled" wines.

The Wine Rack

Church & Wellesley, Toronto, ON
Canada

DESIGN   Shikatani Lacroix, Inc., Toronto, ON

Shikatani Lacroix Inc., the Toronto-based firm, created this simple, clearly defined wine and spirits store called The Wine Rack. In an oddly shaped space of approximately 700 sq. ft., the wines and liquors are lined up in wall modular cabinets set up on the diagonally laid ceramic tiled floor. Dominating the floor is the natural maple and terra cotta laminated cash/wrap desk.

The wall cabinets, 7 ft. 4 in. x almost 4 ft. wide are outlined with stained maple uprights and they carry the adjustable shelves covered with a clear maple laminate. The 17 in. natural maple overhead storage bins are lined in stained walnut and the gray/green lattice frames highlight the classification signage. The same mossy green serves as an accent on the cabinet pulls.

To open up the rather low ceilinged space, the walls and ceiling are painted a warm off-white, and the ceiling is patterned with recessed, baffled fluorescent fixtures and track lights lined up along the cabinets on the perimeter walls. They provide the warm and flattering accent light for the stocked bottles. Windows, along two sides of the site, provide full visibility into the store as well as allow daylight to stream in.

A low crate unit with the low shelf angled for better product visibility is lined up under one of the windows. Merchandise is displayed on top of the unit to entice shoppers on the street. Custom designed angled "crate" displayers appear on the floor to show off the new arrivals and featured specials. The light wood finish contrasts with the rich brown color of the flooring.

The Marketplace

Marshall Field, Northbrook, IL

DESIGN *Pavlik Design Team, Ft. Lauderdale, FL*

PRESIDENT/CEO *Ronald J. Pavlik*

DIRECTOR OF DESIGN *Luis Valladares*

DESIGNERS *Fernando Castillo & Placido Herrera*

PLANNER *Cesar Lucero*
For Marshall Field

SR. V.P. STORE PLANNING & DESIGN
Andrew Markopoulos

DIRECTOR OF STORE PLANNING *Jim Seyko*

MANAGER OF DESIGN *Jane Van Auken*

PHOTOGRAPHER *Myroslav Rosky, Rosky & Assoc., Ft. Lauderdale, FL*

The Marketplace, in the lower level of the Marshall Field department store in Northbrook, IL, simulates a Tuscan courtyard. A circular rotunda is the central focal point and radiating out from it are the food and gourmet merchandise "shops." Light colored, fossil stone columns and brass railings help to define the sidewalk cafe style coffee bar.

A basket weave pattern on the floor composed of three different colored marbles "creates a special arrival point for the heart of the Market Place."

Caffe Gio/Gourmet Foods is designed with rich woods, marble floors and the aforementioned fossil stone columns that reinforce the Old World courtyard environment. Gourmet foods are available here.

The Market Place also boasts of a Wine Shop which is adjacent to the sidewalk cafe—Caffe Gio. Arches, set between the columns, further enhance the Tuscany ambience just as the custom painted murals in the dining area recreate the panoramic setting and excitement of an open air Mediterranean market. The Candy Shop is distinguished by its chocolate toned woods and the brass accents. Furniture style tables and vitrines add a "residential" quality to the setting for the gourmet candy presentation.

Napa Valley Gourmet

Rio Suites Hotel, Las Vegas, NV

DESIGN *AM Partners, Honolulu, HI*

Located in the new and exciting Masquerade Village at the Rio Suites Hotel in Las Vegas is the handsome gourmet "convenience/gift/part" shop. Because of the store's challenging space on this dark and frenetic main level, and its having relatively little "storefront" facing the activities, visual displays and effective lighting were used to attract and draw revelers into the shop.

Entering the store is like stepping into a Spanish estate—such as one finds in the Napa Valley vineyard region. The perimeter walls are faux finished to resemble aged stone walls. To further the Napa Valley association, grapes are stenciled above the arched windows. A weathered wood trellis wreathed in grapevines appears overhead and adds an out-of-doors feeling to the shop as does the "spring day" lighting and the pale blue sky ceiling. Two large arches visually delineate the boundaries from outdoors to indoors.

Dark wood beams contrast with the light walls of the interior and the lighting fixtures recall the craftsmanship of master artisans. Adding to the "rustic" flavor of the store are two shallow alcoves with arched wood beams and wrought iron.

The design firm's, AM Partners, "attention to detailing is expressed in the carved walnut panels, corbels and hand crafted wall tiles." The fixtures are finished with distressed woods, wrought iron, and hand glazed tile tops on the cash/wraps. Antique wood barrels embody the appearance and feel of a traditional winery.

Located immediately adjacent to this store is The Wine Cellar which is also shown in this volume.

GOURMET MARKET

Napa Valley Gourmet
Rio Suites Hotel, Las Vegas, NV

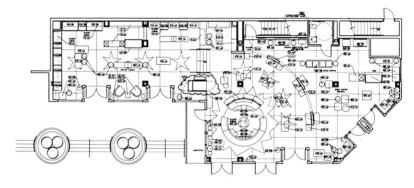

Carnaval Corner

Harrah's Casino/Hotel, Las Vegas, NV

DESIGN   FRCH, Cincinnati, OH

PHOTOGRAPHER   Paul Bielenberg

Conceived as the Las Vegas version of an upscale food market, the 4000 sq. ft. space has entrances on Las Vegas Blvd. and from the casino's central court. This enables the shop to attract resort guests as well as capture street traffic. Designed by the Cincinnati office of FRCH, it is a food/party shop "designed to celebrate the art of eating and drinking as a festive event." More than a convenience store but less than a supermarket, it stocks all the ingredients for a great party including prepared foods, specialty gourmet items, gift baskets and a large selection of wines, spirits and non-alcoholic beverages. With Harrah's private label foods for sale and with cameo appearances from the hotel's chefs, the store also serves as a showcase for the casino's restaurants.

The centerpiece of the store is the juice/coffee bar which is capped with an extravagant plastic fruit cornucopia. The bar is framed by colorful metal ribbons which appear to float in the air above as a giant star made of broken ceramic tiles is inset into the polished concrete floor below. Bright colors, enticing visual displays and bold graphics establish and maintain the upbeat ambience of Carnaval Corner. Large scale vintage signs contrast with the contemporary design of the space and theatrical lighting adds to the party attitude. Colorful globe lights are suspended from the ceiling like helium filled balloons. Gobos

project star patterns on the walls and floors. Customers are even invited to rest in the funky, vinyl alligator upholstered chairs and start "partying" there if they so desire.

A high level of audio/visual stimulation is maintained throughout. Party theme clips from old TV shows such as "I Love Lucy" and "The Three Stooges" are mixed in with vintage footage of food and beverage commercials. The montage of clips appears on monitors located in the most unexpected places such as in the coolers, on shelves, in wire baskets. Meanwhile, filling the space is the sound of eclectic "party" music that spans eras, style and cultures.

FRCH also created an extensive graphics program which includes the "party-to-go box" which can be customized, paper goods and such. It's a great party-to-go place in a place that is partying all the time.

Island Market

Fisher Island, FL

DESIGN *Pavlik Design Team, Ft. Lauderdale, FL*

PHOTOGRAPHER *Myro Rosky*

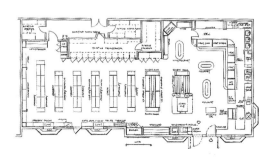

Located on Fisher Island, a private community in Miami's Biscayne Bay, the Island Market was designed "in the fine tradition of European gourmet markets" for the residents of this upscaled area.

The 3500 sq. ft. remodel of an existing store includes a new entrance which incorporates a series of old fashioned bay windows and each window shows off a fabulous display of different epicurean delights. "Shoppers enter into a world of culinary pleasures as they experience the sights, sounds, and aromas of this unique gourmet marketplace." The light and airy Mediterranean feeling of this market was inspired by the historic Vanderbilt Mansion which is a 1920s villa of Mediterranean styling here on Fisher Island

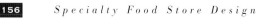

Fossil stone arches, terra cotta tiled floors and polished marble counters trimmed with gleaming brass provide an Old World ambience for the specialty foods. Custom wood fixtures and wrought iron crafted bakers racks hold and display the products. The pendant glass and brass lighting fixtures are incorporated with the signage program.

The signage makes it easy for the first-time shopper to experience the entire elegant presentation of wines, pastries, gourmet prepared take-out foods, and tropical fruits and gift baskets. Shopping Island Market is as upscale and as refined as a food shopping experience gets.

L'Epicure Cafe

Holt Renfrew, Ste Foy, PQ, Canada

DESIGN   *Yabu Pushelberg, Toronto, ON*

PHOTOGRAPHER   *Robert Burley, Design Archive, Toronto, ON*

L'Epicure Cafe is part of the 34,000 sq. ft. Holt Renfrew store in Ste Foy, Quebec. Like the specialty store, "it combines the relaxed and informal 'no attitude' style of the suburbs with the cutting edge fashion and customer service associated with the retailer's flagship downtown (Toronto) location."

The grid concept has been transformed into a wall system used throughout the gourmet food shop. It not only frames the cafe proper but capitalizes on the appeal of the packaged goods massed for presentation. "The simple grid becomes a merchandiser's dream that showcases 50% of the client's branded food goods."

The warm and friendly—and appetizing—environment incorporates limestone counter and table tops with rich dark colored woods and floors paved with limestone—all of which complement the produce and the packaged gourmet items. Racks for fresh baked bread are incorporated into the cash/wrap desk and the point of sale goods are "gracefully" housed behind etched glass partitions.

The seating in the cafe area consists of a curved banquette with tables, some table and chair set-ups and stools pulled up to the Espresso bar. The white walls and ceiling reflect the combination of fluorescent and recessed incandescents in the ceiling on to the light colored stone tabletops and flooring to create an overall light and fresh ambience.

Cafe Europa

Water St., New York, NY

DESIGN *Morris Nathanson Design Inc., Pawtucket, RI*

PROJECT DIRECTOR *Josh Nathanson*

PHOTOGRAPHER *Warren Jagger, Providence, R.I.*

The Water St. location for this Cafe Europa in New York City was selected by the Xenopoulos family because it is in a high foot traffic area and the Prudential Securities building also affords both lobby and street front entrances.

Cafe Europa was designed by Morris Nathanson Design of Pawtucket, RI to be "a high end take-out/restaurant" serving quality prepared foods and baked goods. Of the 3400 total sq. ft., 2000 sq. ft. is used for the front of the house and here presentation and the display of specialty food items are foremost.

The materials used evoke a Mediterranean/European feeling with warm woods, specialty tiles, custom light fixtures, and hand glazed, faux finishes blending to become Cafe Europa's signature look. Another unique part of the design is the black stand-up letters. French bistro tables and chairs provide the loose seating while rich materials and detailing on the banquettes "provide an air of comfort and warmth." The table tops are all mahogany finished.

A patron has several choices in the Cafe Europa. Hot meals are shown on the menu boards and in display cases. There are pastas, pizzas and sandwiches as well. A variety of "cold foods" can be taken directly from the cases and baked goods are shown on the countertops and racks. Though, as previously indicated, interior seating is provided, the real business is the take-out service.

Burke & Burke

Third Ave., New York, NY

DESIGN   *Tree House Design, Ltd., New York, NY*

DESIGNER   *Julius S. "Jack" Baum*

PHOTOGRAPHER   *Stephen J. Carr*

Over a period of time Burke & Burke has established a reputation in its lavender toned stores located around Manhattan for its high quality take-out foods and superior service.

The new owners wanted the public to know that the company would continue to serve them well but they also wanted to establish "new brand identifiers" which could be used in future stores "as a common vocabulary." Instead of the over-generous use of lavender that had been the signature color of Burke & Burke, it is now used primarily as an accent color to highlight the cherrywoods and the multi-colored gray and pinks speckled granite countertops. The floor is a pattern of smooth limestone tiles with solid lavender porcelain tiles as the accents.

This space has a double height ceiling so mezzanines were installed at either end of the store to "create food preparation areas and create activities throughout the store." The ceiling is divided into three bays outlined with finished wood

   Specialty Food Store Design

moldings and sound absorbing panels. A 12 ft. high partition of finished wood and glass separates the service area from the public food display area. This partition passes under the main mezzanine and forms an intimate dining area for about 20 patrons.

The freshly prepared salads and pastries are showcased in display cases of brushed brass and polished stainless steel. Freshly baked breads and pastries are prepared on the smaller of the two mezzanines "filling the entire space with the aroma of fresh baked goods."

Ethel M. Chocolates

Showcase Mall, Las Vegas, NV

DESIGN *The Retail Group, J'Amy Owens*

CEO *Cristopher Gunter*

PROJECT MANAGERS *Cara McClarty, Rob Coburn*

CO-CREATIVE DIRECTORS *Anne Croney, Greg Arhart*

STORE PLANNING *Karen Leemans, Conrad Chin, David Kelly, Greg Moore*

PROJECT ARCHITECT *Cunningham Group, Solbert & Lowe, Marina Del Rey, CA*

GRAPHICS/SIGNAGE *Eunice Chan, Casey Cram*

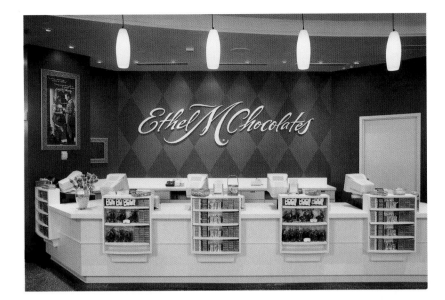

Although Ethel M. Chocolates, a subdivision of the M&M/Mars Corp. has been selling high quality chocolates and confections in 21 stores across the U.S., the brand is not clearly established in the minds of customers. The goal set for The Retail Group of Seattle was to reposition the brand, the product and the packaging to "create a strong, memorable and category differentiating identity for Ethel M. Chocolates."

The entrance, or street level, of the four story, 26,000 sq. ft. space is devoted to providing customers with an emotional connection with the Ethel M. Chocolates that is both romantic and memorable. A focal fixture on this floor is a unit topped by a giant cupid surrounded by mountains of chocolates. In addition to the wide selection of deluxe boxed assortments, customers can customize their own selections in the "Create-Your Own" area. The Ethel M. Packaging repeats the romantic concept of cupids, the life-size photos of classic movie kisses and the chocolate inspired quotes which trail across the ceiling by wrapping the candy in "love letters."

The second floor pays homage to the M&M/Mars brands which include Snickers, Skittles, Mars, Milky Way and—M&Ms. Featured on this level is a 12 ft. Colorworks fixture which dispenses a range of 14 M&M colors. Here too, customers can customize a bag of M&Ms by picking and choosing from the assorted "decorator" colors.

The third floor is an interactive, entertainment based attraction where people learn how "Ms earn their Ms."

From the windows of the fourth level there is a spectacular view of the NY/NY Hotel across Las Vegas Blvd. as well as many other dazzling sights the shopper can enjoy while sampling "a decadent slice of desert" at the Dessert Bar. Also there is an Ethel M. Gallery and an M&M Gallery and a huge M&M bag that seems to be spilling peanut M&Ms onto the cash/wrap desk.

In a city of excessiveness, the M&Ms World facade is a real standout as giant M&Ms cavort over the glass curtain wall—spilling and filling the space.

Peppermint Bay

*Foothills Town Center,
Ahwatukee, AZ*

DESIGN *Miller Rausch, Phoenix, AZ*

PHOTOGRAPHER *David Tevis, Phoenix*

"The goal was to create the sense of being within the candy itself. Nothing was left untouched by the sophisticated and intense colors used in the high energy patterns and forms. The objective was to intrigue the numerous passersby and have them come inside." Peppermint Bay is a new retail concept of the Delstar Group and this prototype is just under 1000 sq. ft.

The space is narrow. The curving floor pattern "like a multi-colored piece of taffy," serves to unify the space and accentuate the width of the store while visually cutting down the length. Also breaking up the length is the organically shaped, vari-colored cash/wrap which serves as a display for candy and also integrates refrigerated cases. It, too, serves as a symbolic piece of candy.

The designers at Miller Rausch, based in Phoenix, designated the checkerboard walls to serve as a "bold attraction for the eye" as well as a background for the bulk candy housed in custom plexiglass bins. A fluorescent green band wraps around the walls at the ceiling. To add to the candy spirit of the concept, the spiral wrapped ductwork with its two tone stripes resembles a giant peppermint stick. Standard black wire framed fixtures were used but the patterned wood turnings and fronts make them unique. The custom, over-sized wheels facilitate constant change on the floor. The displays have specially designed millwork storage cabinets for on-the-floor storage and the curved fronts catch falling candy.

This project has received the top award for Design Excellence from the Southwest Chapter of the International Interior Design Association.

FAO Schweetz

Watertower, Michigan Ave., Chicago, IL

DESIGN *J. Newbold & Assoc., Inc., New York, NY*

DESIGNER *Joanne Newbold*

GRAPHIC DESIGN *John Kehe*

PRODUCER OF CONSTRUCTION
DOCUMENTS *AAD, Phoenix, AZ*

ARCHITECT *Timothy Pleger*

The new FAO Schwarz concept store—FAO Schweetz—is a "dream come true for kids of all ages—a candy heaven on earth." This store design which either shares space with the noted toy store or stands alone as it does in the Watertower in Chicago, is a treat for all the senses. It is bright color, fun, imagination, animation, lights and wonderful sweet delights in bulk containers or pre-packaged for easy shopping.

The floor is laid out like a giant Candyland playing board with colorful blocks of tiles snaking in and around the floor fixtures that are also colorful and bright. Up near the front is a nine ft. tall chocolate soldier and a gummy bear totem pole. The adventure filled stroll through this "giant gumball machine" takes the shopper through a lollipop forest and past a chorus line of Jolly Belly Beans strutting their stuff as they highlight the myriad flavors of jelly beans in the glistening glass cylinders beneath them. The three dimensional, animated "gummy aquarium" is designed to look like a giant diving helmet. Here, "gummy fish, sharks, worms, and other creepy crawly creatures provide delicious bait for the unsuspecting candy divers."

M&Ms Colorworks™ prominently appear in FAO Schweetz with a rainbow of 24 individual colors highlighted by new "stars" in gold, silver, pink, aqua and lavender. Two animated M&M characters carry on a fun-filled conversation to the delight of the children held in rapt attention.

For the serious choco-holic there is FAO Schweetz Chocolate Mint where "gold bricks" of Godiva Chocolates are contained in a "vault" guarded by a chocolate soldier. The vault carries the "Godiva at FAO Schweetz" signage and it signifies a first for Godiva and will probably lead to a line of co-branded products.

Forty four different flavors of "sours" are found in the Sour Patch Fruit Stand. Bushel baskets and seed-packet signage—along with talking sour faced characters "redefine the concept of a sour-face." The adventure ends—as all games must— at the Weigh-In Station: the checkout counter. The scale makes a loud announcement full of hoots, toots, whistles and shouts—based on how much candy is being weighed. It makes a fitting and fun finale for the entertaining experience and best of all—there is still the candy to be eaten at leisure.

This design has won numerous design awards for its colorful, imaginative and unique solution for a store design under 5000 sq. ft.

Sweet City

DESIGN *Triangle Design, Canada*
Jean Jacques Bouchard

PHOTOGRAPHER *Steve Budman*

Sweet City shops, usually located in spaces 600-800 sq. ft. in size, are found in many malls across the country. The design concept, created by Jean Jacques Bouchard of Triangle Design, is meant to suggest the "city" in the store's name. By using clear acrylic shaft-like bins and tubes, not only are the candy's colors and textures maximized, but the container shapes recall a city skyline.

In addition to the "urban" look, the store features pavement markings, cranes and other city sights.

Each store stocks from 500-700 different candies and sweets from all over the world in bulk. Sugar-free, low calorie and sodium-free candies are featured. In addition, there are balloons and specially-wrapped seasonal packages that add to the festive street fair look of the store. Even jelly beans are mixed and matched in NFL team colors to suit the site of the store.

Sweet City Express is a free-standing, candy dispensing unit designed to be located in other stores such as ice cream shops, video rental operations, etc. A mini-version of the in-line candy store, the colorful candy collection is also showcased in acrylic "towers" that emulate a city skyline. In this self-service situation, the shopper picks, packs and weighs the purchase and then pays at the host store's cash desk.

Candy Lab

Uptons, N. Dekalb Mall, Decatur, GA

DESIGN *Fitzpatrick Design Group, New York, NY*

PHOTOGRAPHER *Jen Fong, Brooklyn, NY*

Uptons, in the North Dekalb Mall in Decatur, GA, is well positioned—"not as a discounter nor a department store—but somewhere in between." It was envisioned by David Dworkin of the Upton's team as "a classic environment loaded with great fashion merchandise, offering outstanding service for the appreciative customer."

Certainly "appreciated" by the children who come along on the shopping excursions is the fun world of the Candy Lab. Located in the Children's department and adjacent to the character arcade is this white, light and shining bright area where the stocked colorful candy is the visual as well as taste attraction.

The walls are painted a luminous white satin and the ceramic aisle leading to and surrounding the Candy Lab is unpolished ebony accented with unpolished gold tiles. All the fixtures are finished with either white laminate or a laminate resembling hardrock maple. Metal accents and sharp lighting make the candy sparkle and glitter.

The biggest challenge to the Kiku Obata design company was to make this 1000 sq. ft. candy store stand out. It had to be unique in its mall location to attract attention, sell merchandise—and be memorable.

The themed concept that was devised for this store relied on three animated characters—Kar Mel Icky, Sterling Sticky and Miss Divinity Goo. They became the "company's founders"—and the company became the theme.

The store is targeted at both children and adults alike who each react differently to the humor of the theme. Bright colors and the playful images enhance the whimsy of the theme. There are references to the "corporate image" used throughout the space like the roll top desks, the three "board room" portraits of the "founders," special chandeliers and the company logo inlaid in the floor at the entrance to the store.

Icky, Sticky & Goo

South Hills Village Mall, Pittsburgh, PA

DESIGN *Kiku Obata & Co., St. Louis, MO*

DESIGN TEAM *Kiku Obata, James Keane, AIA, Jane McNeely, Sylvia Teng, Tim McGinty, Idie McGinty*

PHOTOGRAPHER *Ed Massery*

Index by Design Firm